A semi-autobiographical account of how a working lad who left school in 1958 with no educational qualifications became a Psychiatric Nurse, and went on to some senior roles within the NHS.

This is a light-hearted account of the progress of the main character through his three years training, and also the strong camaraderie which existed in the mental hospitals in the early 1960s. This, very sadly, seems to have largely been demolished at the same time as the hospitals! But – read on!!!

Be prepared to laugh frequently, and also, more rarely, to cry!

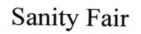

Sanity Fair

Ivor James

Sanity Fair

Vanguard Press

A CIP catalogue record for this title is
available from the British Library.
ISBN 978-1-80016-534-2

Vanguard Press is an imprint of
Pegasus Elliot Mackenzie Publishers Ltd.
www.pegasuspublishers.com

First Published in 2023

Vanguard Press
Sheraton House Castle Park
Cambridge England

Printed & Bound in Great Britain

To Dinah (Di) Wilkinson (11th June 1946 to 10th December 2021) for all her hard work in transcribing the original typescript into MS Word. God bless you Di.

Teresa Cruwys, for all her help and encouragement in finishing the book.

Prologue

Sanity Fair is a book that I had been trying to write for many years, but trivial matters like attempting to make a living, marital difficulties and, at times, indolence, kept getting in the way.

Whilst the book affords a mainly light-hearted description of my entry into psychiatric nursing, my subsequent training in my late adolescence and a number of experiences that I underwent, it was written against a background of almost continual, politically motivated and largely non-productive changes in the management of hospitals in the last four decades of the twentieth century. These interruptions continue to this day, throughout the NHS and other public services, and whilst there have been some improvements over those years, they were often very long-drawn-out developments which produced marginally better care.

I do not criticise the people charged with making these changes, or even the politicians who demand them with each new Government. But! The very fact that these changes arise from political expediency is a very large part of the problem. Governments have a limited life span between elections, whilst reorganising the ways in which hospitals are managed, built, staffed and financed takes decades. If a decision is made to build a new District General Hospital today, it will be at least twenty years before the first patients are admitted. Local consultations, the obtaining of wayleave and planning permission, decisions regarding the clinical content of the proposed hospital, and long delays in securing the initial capital outlay and ongoing revenues cannot, it seems, be hurried.

In the 1970s and '80s, a number of enquiries into some very bad practices and poor management in a number of hospitals for the mentally ill, and the 'mentally handicapped' (these nomenclatures start off with the best intentions but eventually become terms of abuse!) resulted, after many years of in-depth inquiries into what had gone wrong and why, in a White Paper named 'Better Services for The Mentally Ill'. Its main proposition was that the – by then – very tired and outdated Georgian and Victorian mental institutions should be closed, and replaced by modern, liberalistic services based in the community. And that, I am afraid, is the point in time when things went from bad to seemingly impossibly worse!

The old buildings were, of course, increasingly difficult and expensive to maintain, and in many cases, their facilities fell far short of even a modest standard by the 1960s. Many of them had been built as 'Houses of Industry' in the late Georgian and early Victorian eras. A visit to one of the now preserved workhouses will give a picture of what conditions then were like. Poor sanitation, internal brick walls painted over rather than plastered, usually in a forbidding dark-green colour, large high-walled yards known as 'airing-courts' and strict separation of the sexes, and children from parents, provided an atmosphere of never-ending gloom and despondency.

From the year 1601, responsibility for the provision of 'poor relief' fell to the local parishes. As the years progressed, the concept of the 'deserving' and 'undeserving' poor developed. The 'deserving poor' were those who were clearly unable, due to various things such as illness, birth defects or the newly coined word 'insanity', to earn a living by working. The 'undeserving poor' were the wastrels and scroungers who simply chose not to work. There is no doubt that over the three hundred or so years of their existence, the workhouses saved many hundreds, if not thousands, from starvation and exposure.

The workhouses did not appear until about 150 years after the 'Poor Law'. By that time, the parishes were beginning to find that the houses they were able to provide for the poor were becoming increasingly overcrowded and derelict. Also, there was the growth of unease amongst the better off that so many families were being deprived of decent housing, and this led to pressure on the parishes to rectify the situation. The workhouses (often referred to as 'Unions'— built by groups of parishes) also conveniently hid the poor from the better off.

There was little understanding of the term 'insanity' until the mid to late Victorian age. The usually adopted concept of there being a clear division between sanity and insanity began to be challenged. It was noted, however, that many of the 'deserving poor' could be easily slotted into the 'insane' bracket. In truth, of course, there is no dividing line, but many shades of grey. Many of the then described 'undeserving poor' had psychiatric disorders, and so, perhaps, were wrongly categorised.

By the mid-19th century, the asylums began to be built. The word 'asylum' means 'a place of refuge', just as today, many people from the developing countries seek 'political asylum' in Britain and many other states.

The origins of the development of the asylums are what gave rise to the still extant stigma surrounding mental illness. That stigma is endemic. I will return to this issue later.

Also, around the end of the 19th century, enlightenment about mental illness began to grow. John Connolly, William Tuke and others began to advocate a more liberal and humane approach to the care and treatment of the insane. The asylums became increasingly 'medicalised' and their Boards of Governors began to appoint Medical Superintendents. Restraint and isolation of violent patients (as they were now becoming referred to) began to fade into the background, but it was not until the Mental Health Act of 1959 that 'mechanical restraint' was prohibited by law, although 'seclusion', often in a properly appointed padded room, was still in use, but was strictly regulated. Straitjackets fell out of use, as they were seen as being a form of mechanical restraint.

Before the 1950s and following the incorporation of the Mental Hospitals into the NHS in 1947 (they had previously been in the tenure of the local councils), the majority of 'long stay' patients suffered from chronic schizophrenia or one of the several forms of dementia. From about the mid-1950s, a group of drugs known as the Phenothiazines became available and were widely used to alleviate the worst symptoms of schizophrenia. These had an immediate and dramatic effect in that it became possible to discharge many schizophrenic patients back to their homes in the community, and these drugs also helped to make them accessible to rehabilitation, enabling them to live normal lives. The 1959 Mental Health Act was a product of this development. It was revolutionary in introducing the concept of informal admission to a mental hospital. Previously, they had to be 'certified' as insane by a magistrate. This often resulted in them being detained compulsorily for many years, whilst the largest majority of them presented no risk to either the public or themselves. One of the reasons for this was the previously referred to stigma surrounding the whole ethos of the mental hospitals and of mental illness itself. This subject will recur several times in the course of this article. The concept of informal admission, therefore, became the cornerstone of future legislation and changes to the ways in which mentally ill people could be cared for.

Having loosely outlined the development of the early shoots of 'Care In The Community', I now return to the subject referred to in the fourth paragraph above.

The string of major inquiries into the failings of several mental hospitals eventually spurred on the closure of these institutions, which had firstly been raised in the Hospital Plan at the time when Enoch Powell was a very effective Minister of

Health. The main purpose of the plan was to begin to replace the very old real estate which the NHS inherited on is inception. This was also the birthplace of the District General Hospitals which sprang up from the 1960s onwards, and which, as also referred to above, had already been many years in their planning.

In the early 1970s, the NHS was undergoing a severe shortage of nurses as demand for the service continued to increase. An inquiry under the chairmanship of Brian Salmon identified the lack of a clearly defined career path in nursing, the need for better definition of the roles of all the tiers of the profession, and the need for senior nurses who were also managers to undergo properly structured management training at the first, middle and top lines. In considering the job titles then extant, a 'Matron' could either be managing nursing in a 10-bed cottage hospital, or one of the large teaching hospitals such as St Thomas', St Barts or similar. Clearly, there was a huge gap in the levels and types of responsibilities involved. This resulted in the title of 'Matron' disappearing, and the re-grading of many senior nurses as Nursing Officers, Senior Nursing Officers, Chief Nursing Officers, etc, reflecting their respective levels of responsibility in the new Line Management system.

Whereas previously the Matron had reported to the Hospital Secretary, a new system emerged whereby the top management team of a hospital would comprise a Chief Administrator, a Chief Medical Officer and a Chief Nursing Officer. Finance and the management of support services such as laundry, portering, catering and maintenance of buildings and equipment became the domain of the Chief Administrator; nursing care standards and the management and training of nurses was the territory of the Chief Nursing Officer and medical policy and postgraduate training of doctors was under the auspices of the Chief Medical Officer.

Alongside the Salmon Report came the 'Cogwheel' report which, on the back of the changes in nursing management, advocated similar line management approaches in all departments and professional groupings. Whilst in most cases this multidisciplinary approach worked reasonably well, the changes in the perceived status of nurses and administrators became a bone of contention which still has repercussions today, although the matter is now somewhat less contentious and is seldom referred to.

Things came to a further head in the 1980s as a result of Sir Roy Griffiths' report into hospital management, which introduced the concept of General Management, identifying a single person as General Manager overseeing all functions and professional groups. This resulted, very sadly, in the decimation of the system of nursing management and the loss, through early retirement or redundancy, of many thousands of senior nurses, who took with them their knowledge, skills and experience as they departed, leaving nurses feeling disenfranchised. Whereas many of the Nursing Officers and above could, and quite often did, take charge of a ward or department, and also monitor the procedures, training, staffing rotas and care plans in a ward, people from outside of the NHS, for example, banks, military service, retail, etc., found themselves trying to run wards and other services for which they were poorly equipped. Nurses were no longer represented at senior management level. This situation has, however, been addressed in latter years.

The inception of General Management also coincided with the demise of the mental hospitals. Most of these had very large estates, mainly due to the fact that prior to them coming into the NHS, the asylums had to be largely self-sufficient in growing and rearing the bulk of the food required, and therefore had farms which were worked by the male patients, whilst the females worked in the laundry, sewing rooms and such.

The farms began to disappear after the inception of the hospital plan. Many became golf courses, and some of the outer fringes began to be sold off. The incoming cohort of general managers looked at these large estates and saw money! Money which could be better utilised, in their view, to improve services in the general hospitals and fund the development of community services. And so, the slaughter began again!

One of the main recommendations of "Better Services for The Mentally Ill" was that there should be a phased withdrawal of hospital services as more Community Psychiatric Nurses were being trained to work away from the hospital environment. This was a 'post-registration' (today 'postgraduate') course for nurses who had worked on wards in the hospitals for two or more years after obtaining their basic qualifications. At this time also, Day Hospitals and Acute Psychiatric Hospitals should be built, the latter on the campus of the local general hospital.

In 1968, a World In Action TV programme focussed upon the very poor state of Powick Hospital, near Worcester. The programme showed woeful conditions in Ward F13, and, as intended, provoked a great deal of controversy. A new management team was appointed, and things at Powick began to improve. Powick was selected to be the pilot scheme testing the recommendations of 'Better Services', and to this day, the NHS denies that 'Man Alive' was a factor in this choice. I had the honour of being appointed Senior Nursing Officer at Powick in 1978, and I worked there until 1984. We did make considerable progress and we learned a lot of valuable lessons. We did realise however, that the proposed transition from hospital to community was no easy task, and all this was documented by the Medical Research Council as we progressed.

As mentioned above though, in the rest of the UK, the incoming general managers decided that they could not wait long enough for all this to happen. They closed the mental hospitals before the services in the community were fully provided. They also sold off the estates, mainly for housing.

We had calculated that for every 100,000 population, there would be approximately 150 people per year who would need ongoing inpatient care. There was a golden opportunity to keep back a small area of ground on each hospital estate for the building of long-stay units, which could be staffed by a cohort of personnel who had cared for them in the old hospital and who knew their needs and characteristics. But—it never happened!

Private mental hospitals were built, and we now see that many of them have fallen far short of what was expected of them. We see people sleeping on the streets in increasing numbers, many of whom have serious mental health issues. Even the ones who are lucky enough to have a roof over their heads are often accommodated in boarding houses, and they are barred from staying in their rooms after breakfast until early evening.

The killing of innocent people by seriously disturbed schizophrenics was almost unheard-of while the mental hospitals were in existence. The patients were all known very well by the caring staff, and they were never allowed out without supervision. The suicide rate is also increasing exponentially.

Never mind climate change or the influx of refugees. If there is one thing that Great Britain should be thoroughly ashamed of, look no further than modern-day mental health services! There is an irony that as 'Care In The Community' develops, the care of the modern-day deserving poor is divided between a mish-mash of private, voluntary, NHS and Local Authority organisations. Bringing all this under one roof would make a lot of sense. That's precisely the conclusion the parishes came to two hundred years ago!

CHAPTER ONE

Ivan Reader kissed his mother on the cheek, picked up his sandwich box and walked down the street of red brick terraced houses, on his way to the first morning of his first job. The rain was falling steadily, the fine drizzle that his mother always said 'wet her through'. Mam's unintended catch phrase had always caused Ivan slight amusement, as it had been his experience that any kind of rain tended to produce this effect. Mam was always coming out with these little stock phrases, which Ivan called 'Mam-ese'. If she said that she had 'a touch of Tuffriatis', she meant that she was feeling 'under the weather', whilst any fight, debacle or upheaval in her life became 'absolute kiosk!'

It was the thought of these gems of Mum's use of the English language, plus her earnest advice to her son to wear clean underwear on this first morning of his working life in case you get knocked down or anything, which provoked Ivan into his embarrassing habit of grinning like a Cheshire cat at his innermost thoughts, to the consternation of Mrs Hawkins, their nosy old next-door neighbour, as she passed Ivan on the street that morning. Mrs Hawkins had always thought Ivan was a little peculiar, ever since as a child, he had fallen from the top of her garden wall into the cess pit which the late Mr Hawkins had dug out at the bottom of the garden and into which he emptied the contents of the bedroom commode. Ivan's view of Mr Hawkins' balance of mind had also been somewhat jaundiced, as he could see no logical reason why the old boy could not empty the effluent down the toilet! It was almost as though Hawkins had planned the placement of the pit to prevent the local lads from indulging in their sport of 'cat walling', which consisted of crawling along the coping bricks of the garden walls which both separated and inter-connected the miles of adjoining courts and back yards of which Derfield was mostly comprised.

As part of the post war 'lump' of kids leaving school at the end of the 1950s, Ivan had experienced more than a little difficulty in gaining suitable employment. For the last two years of his undistinguished but steady passage through the curriculum offered by the Derfield Secondary Modern School for Boys, he had developed an increasing interest in the technical aspects of radio and television, spurred on by 'Stinks' Rowley, his enthusiastic science master, who encouraged all the boys in Ivan's class to build a simple radio set, utilising the recently invented and somewhat mysterious transistors. Ivan's conviction that the radio and television repair business was for him had been bolstered by the fact that his set was the only one in the class which actually worked, including the one which 'Stinks' had built as a model for all the others! Ivan had ignored the comments of his fellow pupils that this was more the work of divine providence than any natural ability on his part and had gone on to build better and bigger sets, to the amazement of himself, his parents and his friends. His happiness was completed when he subsequently landed a job as an apprentice with the small firm whose premises he was now legging it towards.

Reaching his goal, he knocked at the door of the firm's main workshop, a broken-down former corner grocery shop. If he expected the door to be flung open wide by a grateful television engineer, who would embrace him like a long-lost brother, he was about to be sadly disappointed. He knocked several times, producing no response. As the time was now nine o'clock, the hour at which he had been instructed to report, he began to wonder if he had come to the right place. He was about to look round the back of the building when an ancient Ford 8 van chugged and rattled into the yard at the side of the shop. With a loud creaking of rusty hinges, the door of the van opened, and a chubby, balding middle-aged man emerged.

"Ello, you the new lad?" the driver of the mobile rust heap inquired.

"Yes, er, that is I'm Ivan Reader. Mr Keeler told me to report to a Mr Smith this morning"

"Oh. I see! So, you're Ivan Reader, are you? You didn't seem very sure. I'm Alf Smith, the Foreman." He offered his hand in greeting to the bemused Ivan and grinned. He liked his bit of fun, did Alf.

"Now then, Ivan, I'll show you your equipment. Come with me young un," He grinned again wickedly and beckoned to Ivan as though he were the spider inviting the fly into his parlour.

Alf led the way into the gloomy interior of the shop, which he partly brightened by pushing a plug into a lethal looking two-pin socket on the wall, causing a strip light over the untidy bench to flicker into life. The sight of the bench was Ivan's second disappointment of the morning. He had half expected to see rows of test instruments on shelves operated by a dedicated team of technicians, bent on solving the myriad technological problems of the age. What he in fact saw was a naked TV chassis surrounded by an assortment of junk, and a solitary multipurpose test meter. An ancient electric soldering iron lay on the splintered plywood surface of the bench, which bore testimony in its charred surface to Alf's habit of chain smoking.

"When do the others arrive?" Ivan asked, in all innocence.

"What others?" came Alf's rhetorical reply. "There's only me and thee, and I'm not so sure about thee!" he said cryptically. "Fred Keeler usually comes in about ten and spends the rest of the morning trying to grope his secretary, who has recently informed him that she's not having any more, which makes a change from trying to avoid his wife, who never seems to have enough. All these frustrations tend to make Fred a little 'tetchy' in the mornings, which leads to him sacking apprentices at the drop of a hat. That's why you're here. The other lad only lasted a fortnight."

Ivan cringed inwardly as he considered the possibilities of what he had got himself into. His expectations of life in the radio trade were already somewhat dented, and they were about to be bent a little more.

"I'll show you your equipment now," said Alf, motioning our hero into the back room of the shop. Looking around him, Ivan identified an old stone sink, surmounted by an equally old brass tap. To the left of the sink stood a Victorian gas stove, whilst a row of chipped and dirty mugs, a rusty tin full of damp sugar, a tea caddy, a kettle and a battered aluminium teapot completed the remainder of the catering equipment provided by Mr Keeler for the restoration of the tissues of his employees.

Alf opened a cupboard, and indicated a broom and dustpan, which lay within.

"And all this, my boy, is yours. Do not betray the sacred trust which is this day thrust upon you." He made sweeping gestures to illustrate his point. "Perform your duties of making the tea, sweeping up and generally acting as my willing slave with diligence and pride, and I might just be able to resist the temptation to kick your arse at every opportunity. I am not known for my tolerance of incompetence, but I will give you fair warning when you are about to incur my wrath."

Ivan grinned. He liked Alf's sense of humour, which so far appeared to be similar to his own. Despite the paucity of the firm's facilities, he had an idea that he was going to get on well in his new career.

Ideas and reality, however, are not always as one, as many have discovered down the ages. The one blot on the escutcheon of his carrying out of his duties as prescribed by Alf, was Ivan's fear of heights. For those of us who go about our business with both feet firmly on the ground, such a phobia can be regarded as being of mere nuisance value, a minor cross to bear, as is, for example, a fear of spiders, to one who occasionally espies a hairy member of the genus Arachnid crawling across the bottom of the bath. Such a dislike of the spinners of webs to the dedicated Entomologist is, however, a decided disadvantage. And so it was with Ivan. He had not thought, at the outset of his chosen path, that television sets require aerials for their proper function, and that the erection of suitable antennae for the purpose involves the installer of such apparatus in the frequent scaling of heights to affect their attachment to chimneys etc.

A few weeks after his entry into the trade, Ivan found himself having to face up to his fear, as it had become necessary for him to adopt the role of aerial rigger, due to an exacerbation of Alf's old back trouble. All would have been well had not Mr Keeler insisted on accompanying Alf and Ivan, on the occasion of their installing a set for his aunt. The old lady lived in a rose covered cottage in the country and doted upon her nephew who also doted upon his aunt. Some said that Fred's dedication to the old lady was motivated by a desire to become a major beneficiary in her will, but Fred dismissed such uncharitable dissertations as the 'sour grapes' of other members of his family who laid claim to the folding stuff which would one day surely come his way.

In the midst of all the aforementioned doting, Fred suggested to the old lady one day that a television set might help her to while away the lonely hours. The Grande Dame had expressed some reservations at first, as she had, on the rare occasions when she may be invited in to watch a programme on embroidery, or all-in wrestling. Fred assured his aunt that he would guarantee to secure faultless reception, giving a bright, clear picture. He had offered to install the set at his own expense, and this had persuaded the old dear to accept his gift with the good grace which befitted the occasion.

The situation of the rose covered cottage at the bottom of the valley made the achievement of Fred's rash promise of faultless reception a little difficult, to say the least, as the signal from the transmitter was very weak. This factor necessitated the erection of a large, double banked aerial array, with a booster amplifier at the head of the ten-foot mast, which in turn had to be attached to the chimney. The task was made doubly difficult for Ivan by the position of the garden fence, leaving little room in which to place the foot of the ladder. Add to this his nervousness at having his efforts observed by the critical eye of the Boss, and it comes as no surprise to find our hero was not happy.

Having already made a somewhat perilous journey to the top of the ladder to secure the chimney lashing harness, Ivan was half-way up, with the aerial over his shoulder, when the ladder started to teeter backwards. Ivan, in fear for his life, dropped the aerial and grabbed the chimney, occasioning grievous bodily harm to the delicate structure of thin aluminium tubing.

This mishap caused Fred to lose his temper, and he set about Ivan in the manner of one possessed. In the course of the ensuing discussion, Ivan suggested to Fred a novel way in which he might dispose of the broken aerial. Fred, who despite his faults had the cool reasoning power of the self-made businessman, decided that to follow Ivan's suggestion would be ungallant, as well as being anatomically impossible. His response was to sack Ivan on the spot!

Having survived the distressing experience of breaking the news to his parents, Ivan was then faced with the problem of finding another job in an overcrowded labour market. He drew a complete blank as a result of his efforts to re-enter the radio trade, which was either another result of the post war 'bulge' or was due to the fact that Fred 'had spread the word'. He therefore decided to look for something completely different, but after several weeks of polite and not so polite refusals, he would have taken a job as a wringer

— outer to a one-armed window cleaner. It was with some relief then, that he eventually landed a job as a trainee machine operator in a lace factory.

Having at last secured suitable gainful employment, pending the arrival of better opportunities in the future, Ivan turned his attention to the solution of another of his fundamental problems. For the last few years, he had been becoming steadily more aware that there was another sex. This astute observation was accompanied by a growing realisation that the aforementioned other sex was markedly different to his own. This fact surprised him for a while, as, being a sound reasoner, he deduced that these delightful female creatures must have always been there! Carrying his hypothesis a stage further, brought the shattering realisation that all that had taken place was that he had reached puberty.

One problem solved often leads to yet another one to be dealt with, and the problem that now confronted Ivan was that he was painfully shy in the company of girls. This was undoubtedly due to a number of factors, i.e. his attendance at an all-boy's school, having no sisters, and the recent development of his awareness of their existence. These difficulties were offset to some degree by Ivan's proficiency as a guitarist in a rock n' roll group. The group had been doing fairly well of late and Ivan had not wasted the opportunity to chat up some of the 'teenyboppers' who followed the group around on their various engagements. This had given him some confidence, but the problem still niggled away at the back of his mind.

His job at the lace works had been interesting at first, but his interest gradually waned as he became more skilled in operating the machine. It is a well-known fact that what is novel today becomes commonplace tomorrow, and so it was with his job.

There was, within the textile industry generally, and the lace trade in particular, a remarkable propensity for longevity amongst the workers. What this was due to, no- one knows, but it is a fact that there were many men working full time in the trade into their seventies and eighties. Most of these gentlemen had been watching the wheels of industry turning from the age of fourteen and they displayed a certain pride in the fact that they had never been unemployed or tempted to take up another trade in all those years, even during the lean times of the 1920s and thirties.

Whilst the attainment of such an unbroken record was of paramount importance to these chaps, Ivan found considerable difficulty in fostering a similar ambition for himself. The thought of walking slowly up and down the platform of the lumbering cast iron leavers frames — "Leavers" after John Leavers, the inventor of the lace frame — for another fifty or sixty years loomed in front of Ivan in much the same way as Marley's ghost haunted Scrooge. This gloomy prospect began to play on Ivan's mind to the degree whereupon it seemed to take on gigantic proportions.

"Strewth!" he thought one afternoon.

As the catch bars pushed the carriages through the warps for the ten thousandth time that day. The reader can be forgiven for thinking that Ivan's utterance was not much to write home about, as cries of exasperation go, but this simple display of emotion marked a turning point in our lad's young life.

"Whatdd'ya mean '*strewth*'?" asked Walter, the octogenarian with whom Ivan was currently bound apprentice.

"I was just thinking, Walter," Ivan began, with the look of the ardent philosopher, "that if I have to spend the rest of my life doing this job, I'll go bananas."

Walter put down the meat pie he'd been savouring, picked up a broken thread and looked at the boy earnestly.

"Now you listen to me, my lad," he said, seriously. "This trade's been good to me, and many others, for more years than I care to remember, and it will be just as good to you. I've seen the time when men fought with each other at the gates to queue for a job here. You ought to think yourself lucky." He turned to the machine and replaced the broken thread, bristling with self-righteous indignation.

Ivan picked up his dirty enamel mug of cold tea and pondered on Walter's words. The old man was patrolling the platform of the machine for which they shared responsibility, looking like Canute as he sat on the beach. He had pushed back the waves of time very well so far, but even he knew that one day they would start lapping round his ankles.

Strewth! thought Ivan.

He arrived home at his customary hour of a quarter past six, pulled his motor bike up the step into the garden and entered the back kitchen of the family home.

"Hello love!", said Mam. "Had a nice day?"

"Not bad I suppose," Ivan replied, throwing the haversack which had contained his sandwiches into a corner. He went into the kitchen (bathrooms were not standard in Victorian terraced houses in those days). He stripped to his underpants, and began to wash the powdered graphite, which was used to lubricate the machines, off his body. The fine blue-grey powder had percolated right through his clothes, giving the impression that he had recently emerged from a wild night in a coal house. This ritual bathing took up best part of an hour every night, and he was growing heartily sick of the whole thing.

Mam looked at her son. She worried about him a little, but not so much it showed. He had seemed to like the factory when he had started there two years earlier, but lately, he had been a little sullen when she asked him about it. She knew there was nothing to be gained by pressing the point, so she carried on with her task of cooking the meal for Ivan and his father, who was due home any time now from his job as a bus driver.

Dad arrived home a few minutes later, and Ivan's brother, Keith, came in from his knock about game of football in the street. The family sat down together for tea and engaged in the half sentences in which families are able to communicate with more understanding than strangers can achieve in a thousand words. Ivan remained silent for most of the meal and excused himself immediately when it was finished. He went upstairs to his bedroom and began to strum moodily on his guitar.

Dad sat by the fire reading the evening paper.

"I wish you'd talk to him," Mam said with a worried tone.

"Talk to who?" asked Dad, over the top of his glasses.

"Our Ivan. Something's worrying him and I don't know what it is. Go upstairs and see him Ike, please."

Ike put his paper down with a sigh. He knew that Mam would not rest until he had talked to Ivan, so he walked up the stairs and entered the boy's bedroom. Ivan was sitting on the edge of his bed strumming a blues chord sequence, whilst Keith lay on his bed reading a comic.

"Go downstairs, Keith." He said sternly. "I want to talk to your brother."

"Aw, Dad!" Keith protested.

"Bugger off!" Dad commanded.

Keith buggered off.

"Now then," Dad began. "What's up with you?"

"Nothing," grunted his eldest son, annoyed at the breaking of his reverie.

"Come off it. Your Mother's worried about you and she keeps getting on to me about it. Now, what is it?"

Ivan looked at his father. He saw the same features in his father's eyes that he had seen in Walter's. Twenty years as a bus driver! Six years of war before that! Another fifteen years to retirement, and then what?

"It's okay, Dad, honestly."

"No, it bloody well isn't!" Ike snapped. He saw Ivan's look of resentment. His tone softened.

"Now look here, son. If there's something bothering you, why don't you tell me? I'll find out eventually. So, we may just as well get it straight now."

Ivan sighed.

"Well, if you really want to know, it's the job. I'm fed up to the back teeth with it. I'd like to have a change, but what else can I do?"

Ike looked thoughtful.

"That bad, is it?"

"Yes! It is, I'm afraid."

"Why don't you do something about it then?"

Ivan looked at his father quizzically.

"Such as what?"

"Look around for something different. What about your interest in radio?" His eldest son still tinkered with the hobby in the garden shed, which had come to resemble a laboratory.

"I haven't got any 'O' levels. They won't take you without them."

"They wouldn't bother about 'O' levels in the forces," said Ike.

Ivan was about to speak, but he suddenly stopped. That was an idea! Why not join the Air Force? They would train him for a trade, possibly even electronics. He would see more of the world than the walls of the lace factory, and he wouldn't come home every night covered in graphite.

"Thanks Dad!" he said brightly and rushed past his astonished father and down the stairs, to join his mates in the coffee bar.

He came home about ten o'clock, whistling and cheerful. He entered the small living room and gave his mother a playful smack across the rump as she was bending over, rummaging in her sewing box.

"What's got into you, then?" she smiled.

"Nothing much. Must be the stuff they put in that coffee. What's for supper?"

Mam went onto the kitchen to make a sandwich for Ivan. Ike hadn't told her what he had said to their son, but it appeared to have done the trick. She slept well that night.

Ivan played 'hooky' from the factory the following day and presented himself at the Royal Air Force Recruiting Office.

"What do you do now, old chap?" asked Warrant Officer Brown.

"I make lace," Ivan replied.

"Oh yes," Brown said warily. "And what else are you interested in?"

"I play the guitar," Ivan muttered, feeling silly after he had said it.

Brown regarded him with an amused smile.

"Oh, yes?" he answered, sarcastically, "well, you see, the trouble is that we don't really need many guitar playing lace makers in the Royal Air

Force. Is there anything else that you might have in mind?"

Ivan thought for a moment.

"I'm interested in radio and electronics," he said, brightening in the way Newton must have done when the apple fell on his head.

"Ah! Now we're talking," Warrant Officer Brown said, with rather more enthusiasm. "How many 'O' levels do you have?"

"None," replied Ivan

"Ah!" said W/O Brown.

"Hm!" Ivan answered.

"Yes, well," from Brown.

This erudite conversation came to an abrupt stop at this point, whilst Brown shuffled through some papers on his desk. Ivan, realising that the RAF had managed to survive the Second World War and Korea without him, began to feel that they could probably carry on for a while longer. He said as much to the warrant officer. Brown found the piece of paper he had been looking for, peered at it, and then at Ivan.

"Well now, look here old boy, we may be able to offer you something after all. Now, assuming that you are interested in training for a trade amongst the old dials and switches, you will definitely need to go for our equivalent of the old 'O's and A's' what? This should take around three years or so. You'll probably need to spend another three years trade training, assuming a wizard crop of 'certs' from the first show, savvy?"

Ivan nodded the nod of one bemused.

"Righto!" Brown went on. "Now then, it might be a good idea then to do another three years to gain oneself a little rank etcetera, and make sure of the old pension scheme, what?"

"Ah!" Ivan said.

"Quite!" Brown replied.

Ivan looked thoughtful.

"Isn't there anything shorter?" he asked. The thought of nine years compulsory detention was a little daunting for him but not as daunting as fifty years in the factory.

Brown smiled.

"Well, old fruit, there is one thing. Tell me, have you ever thought about becoming a nurse?"

Ivan smiled at the thought of himself resplendent in a frilly cap and snow white 'pinny', dispensing Aspirins and bed pans to wounded 'types' with large moustaches and overdone Oxford accents.

W/O Brown, noting his amused expression, leaned over the desk and spoke in serious tones.

"No, seriously old boy," he began, "we need more chaps to train as Psychiatric nurses, and hefty lads like yourself are just the ticket, what?"

Remembering that one of his objectives in life was to conquer his shyness with the opposite sex and having seen a couple of male nurses mincing round the local infirmary, Ivan did not really see W/O Brown's suggestion providing the answer to his problems. He thanked the warrant officer for his trouble, and went away, having assured Brown that he would think it over.

It was with such thoughts in his mind that he returned home that evening, feeling doomed to spend the next fifty years or so at the factory. To counteract his depression, he spent the next couple of weeks or so indulging in the mad social whirl which hung over Derfield like a wet weekend in 1961. He went to the local Palais every night except Tuesday, when he played guitar at the local jazz club, where the audience were comprised mostly of bored teenagers who didn't fancy the 'Old Tyme Night' at the Palais.

This sophisticated existence was occasionally punctuated by a visit to a proper jazz club in a neighbouring town, where the giants of jazz (to Ivan, anyway) played their 'authentic' New Orleans jazz, which had never been heard further west than Llandudno. The fans were consoled by the fact after a few pints of Bass, Johnny Mortimer's 'tailgate' trombone style was almost as good as that of Honore Dutrey.

The rock group, however, was doing reasonably well at this time, and they eventually secured a residency at the first real night club to open its doors in Derfield. At first, it looked as though they were really about to make the big time, especially as they were occasionally asked to back well-known cabaret artistes when the club owner felt brave enough to sink a few quid on engaging them. To their dismay though, they quickly found that most of these artistes demanded a higher standard than they were capable of providing, often having to re-arrange their repertoire to suit the limitations of the band. The big time gradually faded into the sunset like the Lone Ranger on Silver, and sadly the group broke up.

As any gardener knows, seed which is planted without result one year will sometimes grow the following spring. This accounts for the phenomenon of a row of cabbages suddenly producing the odd carrot, and a similar process to this had been taking place at the back of Ivan's mind over W/O Brown's suggestion that he might become a nurse. The more he thought about it, the more it seemed to grow. The spectres of the two mincing gents at the infirmary, however, served like weeds in a cabbage patch. They stifled the young plant and prevented it from growing into more than a stunted replica of the fully grown vegetable. Whilst he imagined that the RAF was a man's life, and that their male nurses were roughly the genuine product, Ivan was still deterred by the prospect of signing on for three, six or nine years.

Things may well have stayed that way, had it not been for a darts match. Having by now developed a marked liking for beer, Ivan had called in at the local one evening to quaff a couple of pints, to find the darts team locked in combat with another side from the Derfield and district league. He knew most of the players in the home side, but he could not recall seeing their opponents before.

In order to understand the ramifications of the situation which Ivan found before him, it is necessary that the reader undergoes, at this point, a short course in protocol which teams in Derfield and District Darts League adhere to like flies to a fly paper. The match itself, the victors of which gain two points in enhancement of their position in the league table, is of secondary importance. But the aspect of the night's contest which has, over a period of almost a century, become paramount, is the winning or losing of the 'beer leg'. (Q.V.)

'BEER LEG' — That portion of the match which is played after the main league match. One player will be selected by each captain to represent his team. The two selected players will play one game, 501 down, the game to commence and finish on a double.

The victorious team will collect, by right of tradition, one pint of beer (or equivalent) each. The cost will be afforded by the losers of the 'Beer Leg'. (Extracted from the rules — Derfield and District Darts League — Established, 1899)

Those readers who are familiar with such contests will appreciate the prestige to be gained by a team who win the beer leg, to say nothing of the beer. The selected player, if victorious, is much revered by his companions, and accorded the status of hero. If defeated, however, he is ostracized, cast out, sent to Coventry and generally reviled. The awesome responsibility borne by these players is not easily discharged. (Uneasy lies the head etc...

On the evening in question, Ivan stepped through the frosted glass door of the saloon bar of the Frog and Pump, to find that the beer leg was just approaching its zenith. The away player was about to throw, with 107 points remaining on the board, the atmosphere in the room was electric, the two teams and the spectators observing the proceedings with bated breath. The player threw, scoring seventeen — single twenty, and losing his last dart, which rebounded from the wire, narrowly missing the landlord.

The home player returned to the oche. A fine glow of perspiration lay on his troubled brow. He had seventy-four points left. He threw a single fourteen, then single twenty, leaving forty, or double top, for his last dart. He threw, missing the board entirely, drawing gasps of dismay from the home crowd.

The away player resumed his stance. He swallowed nervously, as though choked by the lump of apprehension which rose in his throat. An old man at the bar called for a pint, drawing 'Sssshhhh!' from the crowd. The player threw, sending the dart spinning through nine feet of highly charged air. The projectile buried its point in the single twenty. His second again rebounded, this time jeopardising the life of the away team's captain. This left fifty points and one dart. He threw and the dart landed on the bull's eye at the centre of the board. Pandemonium broke loose in the room. The visiting team picked up their hero, carrying him shoulder high through the rear doors of the pub, where they gleefully deposited him on one of the bowls in the 'Gents', pulling the chain whilst they held him in position. They returned to the saloon bar where the home team were morosely 'shelling out' for the beer.

The evening's post-match jollifications progressed rapidly after that. One of the visiting team did battle with the ancient, out of tune piano, and community singing soon set in, as is inevitable as an aftermath of such occasions as this. Ivan now had time to study the visitors a little more closely. They bore some resemblance to the popular image of a Rugby XV, rather than the usual collection of middle aged, bronchitic Woodbine smokers which constituted the nucleus of the average pub darts team. They were all jolly, muscular young men with a sense of humour and friendly attitude, which quickly enamoured them to the regulars of the Frog and Pump.

To say that a good time was had by all would be an understatement, particularly after the visitors had entertained the clientele by singing popular ditties like 'The Ball of Kirriemuir,' 'The Engineers Song', and 'The Virgin Sturgeon'. An old chap sitting next to Ivan was particularly amused by the recital which the lads provided. He had joined in with their rendition of 'Roll Me Over' with such gusto that they had pulled him to his feet and persuaded him to sing a solo. This he did with great relish, treating his audience to a moving rendition of 'Smiling Through' during the course of which he changed key three times, finishing with a paroxysm of coughing which was drowned by the thunderous applause.

After resuming his seat to regain both his breath and composure, he turned to Ivan and said, "They're a right bloody sample, aren't they?"

Ivan agreed with this observation, remarking that they reminded him of a bunch of all in wrestlers on their night off. This statement produced from the old man a burst of laughter, followed by a violent attack of coughing, after which he turned a deep purple colour and made noises like water going down the plug hole of a bath.

"Ay up mate, he's choking!" shouted one of the visitors.

Before Ivan could bat an eyelid, the dart player seized the old man and threw him across a chair, face downwards. He clouted the pensioner between the shoulder blades, expelling a wedge of pork pie from the old man's gullet. The old boy burped, coughed, wheezed and sat up, assisted by Ivan and the chap who had performed the resuscitation. He sat in the chair drawing in great lungs full of air, wheezing like an out of tune harmonium.

"Whew, thanks mate!" he eventually gasped. "I thought I was a goner then."

"That's all right, Pop," said his saviour, "it's all part of the service. Let me buy you a drink."

"No bloody fear!" said the old man. "I'll buy you one." He turned to Ivan. "And you'll have one as well."

"I'll settle the argument," Ivan said. "I'll buy a round for all of us." He stepped over to the bar before either of his companions could protest further.

Ivan took the drinks back to the table, where the old chap was in conversation with his rescuer and one of the other members of the visiting team.

"It's a bloody good job these blokes were here," he said to Ivan.

"Why is that?" Ivan asked.

"They're all male nurses," the old man said, and laughed so hard that the three younger men feared for his life once more.

"How are you, Ivan?" the newcomer asked. Ivan looked up sharply at his face, and recognised him as Peter Johnson, an old school chum.

"Okay, thanks Pete," Ivan replied, shaking Pete's hand with happy surprise.

They exchanged memories of schooldays, interspersed with enquiries as to where 'old so-and-so' had got to, and what 'old what's-his-name' was doing for a living, and all the usual conversation which takes place when old friends meet after a long separation.

"Is that right that you're a male nurse?" Ivan asked Pete, at length.

"Yes, that's right," Pete grinned back. "Are you surprised?"

"I am really. I wouldn't have thought that you were the type."

"Oh yeah! And what do you think the 'type' is?" Pete asked, suspiciously.

"Oh! No offence, but I've only seen those two left-handed five bob notes at the infirmary."

"Ah! You mean Gerald and Clarence!" said Pete, as the realisation of what Ivan's image of what the male nurse must be dawned on him. "Don't take those two bloody fairies as an example. We're all Psychiatric nurses at the Meadows. That's a different set up all together."

Ivan apologised to Pete for any offence which his remarks may have caused.

"No need, no need at all," said Pete. "Most of the public never see the inside of a mental hospital, so they can't be expected to know what goes on."

"But I always thought of the Meadows as the workhouse," Ivan said.

"Another popular myth!" Pete exclaimed. "It's a modern, go-ahead Psychiatric unit. Most of the people who are unfortunate enough to be admitted there don't stay for more than a few weeks. By that time, they're completely well again, and are ready to go home and back to work. It wasn't always like that of course. Most of the progress has only been made in fairly recent times, but progress there most certainly has been. I like the job. It's interesting and varied, and we have a darned good social life, as you can see." He pointed around the room, indicating his colleagues, most of whom were now well and truly 'in their cups'.

The rogue plant in Ivan's mind suddenly bore fruit, and he told Pete about Warrant Officer

Brown's suggestion that he should become a Psychiatric Nurse.

"Why not?" Pete asked. "You don't need to join the Air Force though - we have an intake of lads and girls of about our age three times a year, look, if you're really interested, why not come and have a look around? I could arrange for you to see Mr Hunting, the Chief Male Nurse, and he could interview you there and then."

"Did you say, girls?" Ivan asked, suddenly more interested.

"Too true!" said Pete, grinning. "That's another reason why I like working at the Meadows."

"It's certainly worth thinking about," Ivan said, already deep in thought.

"Well, you will have to make up your own mind. It's one of those jobs that only you can decide on. Think it over for a few days, then if you want to follow it up, ring Mr Hunting on this number." He scribbled a telephone number on the back of a beer mat, which he handed to Ivan.

The next morning dawned rather painfully for Ivan, as is often the case on the 'morning after the night before'. He eventually managed to summon the strength to crawl downstairs for breakfast, wincing as Mam clattered the pots and pans in the kitchen.

"Good grief!" Ike exclaimed, viewing the shattered remains that had once been his eldest son. "Where the hell did you get to last night?"

"I met an old friend," Ivan groaned.

"Looks as though your friend was a brewery." Ike grunted, returning to his paper.

"I've done you a few bacon sandwiches," Mam said, bringing in a plate. "I thought you would like that."

"Thanks Mam," Ivan whimpered, hardly daring to look at the fare which had been offered to him.

Many readers will be familiar with the state of health that we find our hero in at this stage of the story. However, for those virtuous few who have never experienced the symptoms of a hangover, I feel it is my duty to offer some explanation, as my contribution to your undoubted interest in how the other half live.

The symptoms can be mainly listed as a taste in the mouth which some have likened to that of a gorilla's armpit, accompanied by a violently throbbing headache, and an acute feeling of nausea at the sight or mention of food. Paradoxically, if the sufferer can steel himself to actually eat something, he immediately begins to feel better. This simple remedy has saved many people from a horrible lingering death!

Fortunately for Ivan, his father had educated him along these lines on a previous occasion, when his son had first come to realise that to mix the grain with the hop is not conducive to good health and regular habits. This knowledge now stood our boy in good stead, and Mam's bacon sandwiches and hot, sweet tea, cured the malady within half an hour. He eventually felt strong enough to broach the question of his future employment with his parents, despite the lingering feeling that his skull had recently been cleft in two by a mad axeman.

"I think I'll leave the factory!" he said, with the same nonchalant air that Napoleon must have adopted when he informed Josephine that he was about to attack Russia.

"How long have you been thinking about that for?" Ike asked, putting down his paper.

"Oh, for a few weeks now. I don't fancy working there until I retire."

"What else have you got in mind?" Ike queried.

"I don't really know," Ivan replied. "I made some enquiries about the RAF last week."

"I wish that I'd stayed in," Ike said. "I'd have had a pension by now."

He had been demobbed from the RAF in 1946, having attained the rank of Flight Sergeant in charge of the squadron's pool of motor vehicles. He had spent most of the post-war years driving the double decker busses that Derfield Corporation provided as public transport. He had little now to show for this career, except a duodenal ulcer, which occasionally doubled him up with pain. Ivan, thinking about this, could understand his father's sentiments.

Mam came out of the kitchen.

"Are you serious about the Air Force?" she asked, looking worried.

"No, not really, Mam," Ivan said to her relief. "It was just something to think about. But I do feel like a change." Neither parent seemed unduly surprised at this revelation, so he continued. "Actually, I met some blokes who are male nurses at the Meadows last night. I wouldn't mind trying that for myself."

His parents looked at each other in surprise.

"That's where they take Bill Walker, isn't it?" Mam asked.

"I think so," Ike replied. "What do you want to go there for?"

Ivan did his best to explain, but he did not feel that he had entirely convinced them of his intentions. Bill Walker lived further up the street, and unfortunately suffered from periodic breakdowns. He had been carted away by ambulance on several occasions, after screaming and shouting that the Germans were coming. This unhappy spectacle drew shakes of the head and 'tut-tuts' from the neighbours, and whispers of 'he's gone off again, then!' accompanied by 'knowing' looks. This obviously caused Mrs Walker great distress and embarrassment, and Ivan had always felt rather sorry for her. Bill always came back after a few weeks in the Meadows, and Ivan realised that this fitted in with the picture that Pete had drawn for him the night before. He also saw it as an illustration of the stigma and prejudice which Pete had told him the public exhibited over mental illnesses, and he found that the thought angered him.

"Why shouldn't I work there?" he demanded crossly of his father. "Someone has to do the job!"

"Well, it's your life," Ike replied, philosophically, returning to his paper.

Mam went back into the kitchen, shaking her head and muttering 'oh dear, oh dear, I don't know, I'm sure!'

Ivan took his crash helmet from the peg in the hall, wheeled his motor bike out of the back yard, and rode into town to the coffee bar. Pete Johnson was sitting at a table with a strikingly pretty girl.

"Hello Ivan. Thought any more about it yet?" he asked.

"Yes, I've thought about it, but I've not decided yet."

"Well, take your time. Oh, by the way this is Sally." Sally smiled at Ivan, sending his blood pressure soaring.

"Hello Sally!" Ivan said. "Where did you meet this reprobate?"

Sally laughed delightfully.

"I work with him. I'm a nurse at the Meadows!"

Ivan rang Mr Hunting the following day!

CHAPTER TWO

Ivan rode his motor bike towards the Meadows Hospital, feeling something like a nineteenth century explorer coming upon a village in a jungle clearing. He didn't really know what he expected to see. He remembered seeing artist's impressions of Bedlam in the eighteenth century, with people chained to walls, and the public queuing up to make fun of the unfortunate inmates. He had heard lurid tales of padded cells and strait jackets from people who had visited the Meadows, or Derfield County Asylum as it had formerly been called, before the Second World War. All these images combined in his mind's eye, giving him an uncomfortable feeling of apprehension as he rode down the half mile long lane which connected the hospital with the main road. He rode between two red brick, stone capped pillars which flanked the main gateway to the hospital grounds. The gateway appeared to have originally been set in a twelve-foot wall, which had since been demolished.

A notice at the side of a small gatehouse read 'Enquiries'. He stopped the bike and looked through the gate into the grounds. The main part of the building was a large, Victorian edifice, with ivy covered walls, and surrounded by lawns which were edged with brightly coloured flower borders. He dismounted and removed his crash helmet. A symphony of bird song echoed around the otherwise silent grounds, giving Ivan a feeling of tranquillity that he had often experienced when walking in the park early on a summer's morning. He stood there for two or three minutes, taking in the quite unexpected scene of grandeur. Remembering the purpose of his visit, he walked over to the enquiry window and pressed the bell.

An elderly, white haired man in a commissionaire's uniform slid the window open.

"May I help you, Sir?" he asked.

"I'm looking for Mr Hunting's office," Ivan explained.

"Just a moment sir, I'll tell him you're here. What name is it?"

"Ivan Reader. I think he's expecting me."

The lodge keeper picked up a telephone and announced Ivan's arrival to Mr Hunting. He replaced the receiver, and directed Ivan to the Chief Male Nurse's office, inviting him to leave the bike at the lodge, where the old man could keep an eye on it. Ivan walked in the direction that the old man had indicated, following the signposts which pointed the way through the maze of buildings. He eventually arrived at the foot of some stairs where a sign indicated that the Chief Male Nurse's office could be found on the upper floor. He climbed the brightly lit staircase, which was spotlessly clean with highly polished brass handrails. He had expected the hospital to have the familiar antiseptic smell, but this was nowhere in evidence.

A tall, smartly dressed man met him at the top of the stairs and introduced himself as Hunting. He shook Ivan's hand firmly and led him into an office.

The interview continued for twenty minutes or so, during which time Mr Hunting explained the options which were open to Ivan. He suggested that Ivan could start off by being a Nursing Assistant for a couple of months. His role would be to help the trained nurses with the basic care of the patients. This would not entail Ivan undertaking training until he was quite sure that he liked the job. It would also give the staff time to assess his capability. If all parties were satisfied at the end of the trial period, he would be invited to sit an entrance test, success in which would admit him to the training school for a three year's course. If he then passed the final examination, he could apply for the qualification of Registered Mental Nurse, the Psychiatric nursing equivalent of State Registered Nurse in a general hospital.

Mr Hunting asked Ivan what had led to his initial enquiry about nursing as a career. Ivan related his conversations with the warrant officer and Pete Johnson.

"Ah yes." Hunting said. "Peter did mention your name to me. Good lad that. He's been with us for a couple of years now."

"Well now," he continued, "assuming that your references are satisfactory, and you pass your 'medical', we will be able to offer you a job. As you do not have any 'O' levels, you will need to take the entrance exam. It's just a sort of intelligence test really. But perhaps you'd like to look around the hospital first? I'll arrange that for you, and for one of the doctors to examine you before you leave. Good luck, and I hope to be seeing you again soon." He smiled and shook hands with Ivan again. "I'll drop you a line as soon as we are able to come to a firm decision."

Mr Hunting pressed a bell on his desk, and a male nurse in a white coat appeared through another door. Hunting asked the nurse, who he addressed as Bill, to show Ivan over the hospital. He handed the entrance examination and application forms to Ivan, and asked Bill to allow Ivan to use his office to complete them at the end of the tour. He bade Ivan goodbye, and Bill escorted him from the office.

They walked along a corridor and through a doorway which bore the legend 'M6'. Inside the ward, Ivan saw several men sitting in a pleasantly furnished lounge, and there were rows of beds visible through the door of an adjoining room. Bill asked one of the men to bring two cups of tea to his office and led Ivan through a door which was labelled 'Charge Nurse'. The office contained a desk, two chairs, a filing cabinet and a large white cupboard with two doors, which were labelled 'Scheduled Poisons' and 'Non-Scheduled Drugs'. Various lists and charts adorned the walls, along with a few press cuttings and some comic post cards on a notice board.

Bill sat down at the desk and explained that a Charge Nurse was the equivalent of a Ward Sister, and that he was in charge of this ward, Male Six.

"Mind you," he said with a grin, "in charge is not really the right word. I usually work on my own, as most of the lads here can pretty well look after themselves. I'm really only here to give them their medicines, supervise the serving of the meals, and act as a sort of 'Father Confessor' to them. There are those though, who would say I was over-simplifying it."

The man who Bill had earlier placed the order for the tea came in carrying two cups.

"Thank you, Ernest; your reward will be in heaven, my son," said Bill, winking at Ivan.

"If I ever bloody well get there!" replied Ernest, casting Ivan a suspicious glance and glowering at Bill.

"It's being so cheerful that keeps him going," Bill grinned, as Ernest withdrew, muttering darkly. "Anyway kid, drink your tea and fill in the forms, then we'll have a look around. It's not a bad job, really, so long as you never expect to be rich. The first thirty years are the worst."

They seemed to walk for miles. Bill showed Ivan several wards, all of which were homely whilst being spotlessly clean. The patients came in all shapes, sizes and age groups, but none of them looked particularly strange, to Ivan's mild surprise. He still didn't know what he had expected to see, but whatever it was, it had been nothing like this.

A further visit they made was to the Industrial Therapy Unit, where rows of male and female patients sat at benches, fitting metal clips to the ends of rubber straps. Bill explained that the straps would be used in car seats, and that the work was carried out under contract for a well-known rubber manufacturing firm. The firm paid the hospital for the work, and the patients were paid in accordance with their capability. The scheme formed part of the rehabilitation programme, which was designed to prepare patients for discharge into the outside world. Bill told Ivan that after perhaps many years of living a fairly cloistered life within the hospital, people tended to lose the 'habit' of working for a living. This workshop helped them to regain lost skills, and to learn new ones, under the expert guidance of the staff.

Bill then took Ivan to the Occupational Therapy Department, where patients were being supervised in various forms of handicraft and art work by ladies in green uniforms, who Bill referred to as 'OTs' explaining this was short for 'Occupational Therapist' These patients either did not need or were not capable of the more industrial form of occupation, but they derived pleasure from making useful articles, or from learning to paint or draw. They were also encouraged to re-develop their skills in forming social relationships, which many of them had lost either from the effects of their illnesses, or again, the very fact that they had been virtually isolated from society for long periods of time.

Continuing the long trek around the hospital grounds, Bill showed Ivan large groups of men working in the fields at the rear of the hospital. Some of them were digging potatoes, which they then loaded into a trailer which was coupled to a tractor. Other smaller groups were working in the gardens which surrounded the buildings. This hive of industry added to Ivan's surprise, as he had always associated hospitals with lying in bed.

Ivan left the hospital that day with very mixed feelings. He had been deeply impressed by all that he had seen, and he found himself thinking seriously about it as he rode home. Thinking seriously was not one of his most prominent characteristics, and he found the experience a little disturbing.

The reaction of his family to his decision to become a nurse was one of surprise. One of his friends went so far as to warn him that it was a well-known fact that the staff at the Meadows finished up madder than their patients.

Ivan found these bigoted views annoying, as he did with other items of folklore which seemed to exist about the hospital. By the time that Mr Hunting's letter arrived, formerly offering him a post, he had taken to actively defending the name of the hospital whenever he heard it used as an object of derision, which seemed to be far too often to be mere coincidence. He deduced that these reactions in the minds of the public were probably caused by that most feared of all entities, the unknown.

CHAPTER THREE

In his letter, Mr Hunting had asked Ivan to report to 'Male Reception', at seven o'clock on this first Sunday morning of his employment. Ivan had never before worked on a Sunday in his life, and he found it rather strange to be wheeling his bike out into the silent street whilst all around him slept. It also seemed strange to be wearing a suit to work, after the years of oil, fluff and graphite at the factory.

He arrived outside the building marked 'Male Reception' at a quarter to seven. He found a cycle shed at the side of the building, where he left his motor bike. It was with a trembling hand that he pressed the large porcelain button of the doorbell a few seconds later. After what seemed a long delay, a key rattled in the lock of the large double doors, which were opened by a white coated young man.

"Hello." He greeted Ivan. "What can we do for you?"

Ivan coughed nervously.

"Er, I'm supposed to be starting here today."

"Oh well, enjoy yourself," said the young man, as he closed the door in Ivan's astonished face.

Bemused, Ivan rang the bell again.

"I'm sorry," he said, when the young man re-appeared, "what I meant was, I'm joining the staff here."

"Congratulations!" his tormentor said, then he shut the door again.

Ivan began to wonder whether this character really was a nurse, or some deranged soul who had purloined a key and white coat from his guardians. He rang the bell again.

"Now what?" the young man asked, irritably. Ivan flushed. He was getting decidedly 'niggled'.

"Now look," he began. "I don't know whether there has been some mistake, but I have a letter from Mr Hunting asking me to report for duty at seven o'clock this morning. Now, you might at least tell me whether I have come to the right place." He thrust the letter angrily at the male nurse, who glanced at it.

"Oh, I see," the other replied. "You'd better come in then!"

"Thank you!" Ivan snapped.

"Not at all!" the nurse replied, bowing formally. "Follow me, young man." He set off down a corridor, beckoning Ivan to follow him. Ivan's former doubts about the sanity of this character now returned, as the latter now began to laugh loudly, his shoulders heaving. He led Ivan into an office, where he sat down at a desk and guffawed, tears rolling down his cheeks.

"You were right, Pete," he shouted. "He fell for it hook, line and sinker!"

The truth of the situation suddenly struck Ivan, as Pete Johnson appeared from an adjoining room, laughing like a drain.

"I'm sorry, mate," Pete choked, "but we heard you were starting this morning, and Ron here and I couldn't resist setting something up for you." He looked at Ivan's puzzled face and doubled up again.

The humour of the 'trap' that he had walked into now reached Ivan, and he began to laugh too. They were all still laughing a couple of minutes later, when a stern looking man entered the office. Sporting the same white coat as the others, he glared at them wordlessly. The two men stopped laughing immediately and realising this must be the Charge Nurse, Ivan did the same.

"I like a joke too," the Charge Nurse growled, "but not at this time on a Sunday morning. Now get your arses out of here."

"Yes Bob!" Pete and Ron chorused, and motioned Ivan out of the office.

"Hang on a minute," Bob said, and Ivan realised that it was he who was being addressed. "I want a word with you, lad!" The other two beat a hasty retreat, leaving Ivan alone with this cross between an angel of mercy and a marine commando. "Sit yourself down for a minute," the Charge Nurse commanded, and Ivan sat down.

"Now then," the Charge Nurse began. "I'm Bob Bracewell, and I'm the Gaffer."

"How do you do?" Ivan asked. "I'm er ...."

"I know who you are," Bob grunted. "I was told that you were coming."

"Ah! I see!"

"Do you now?" Bracewell said, menacingly. "Right! Let me just put you right on a few points then. Number one, be punctual. Number two, don't do anything without checking with me or Ron first. I'm responsible for these patients and I'm not letting you loose on them until I know a bit more about you. Number three, I do not tolerate an untidy appearance. Number four, you'll work with Ron today, and do exactly as he says. Understand?"

"Yes," Ivan said.

"Good!" he said, then "Ron, come in here and take him away!"

Ron came back into the office, and introduced himself properly to Ivan as Ron Mount, Staff Nurse. He was a slightly built, nervous looking individual, with an accent that Ivan took initially as being Yorkshire. Ron later told him that in fact, he came from North Derbyshire, and had been a miner before coming to the Meadows. He had been forced to change his job when he developed Nystagmus, an eye condition which has terminated many a miner's life underground.

"Mr Bracewell seems to be a strict type," Ivan ventured.

"Oh, he's not too bad, really. You should see some of the others!"

Ivan thought that if Bracewell was 'not too bad' the others must be something to be seen!

They went upstairs into a dormitory which contained about thirty beds. The patients were starting to get up, and some were in the washroom, shaving, at a row of hand basins. One of them came over, dressed in pyjama trousers and carrying a towel.

"Can I have a blade, please Ron?" he asked.

"Hang on for a few minutes, Dennis, and I'll get you one," Ron answered. He pulled Ivan to one side. "That will be your first job," he said. "You'll have to keep an eye on him whilst he shaves. I'll fetch the blades up and give them to you. If any of them ask you for one, watch them like a hawk. We don't want any problems, do we?"

Ivan looked puzzled.

"What sort of problems?" he asked.

Ron looked at him despairingly.

"Look, mate," he whispered, "some of these are in here following suicide attempts. Others are here for doing nasty things with knives. Now do you see why we have to be careful?"

Ivan gulped.

"Er, yes, I think so."

Ron nodded.

"Good. Now keep an eye on things for a couple of minutes while I get the blades." He went downstairs, leaving Ivan feeling like a fish out of water.

Dennis walked over to him.

"Don't let what he says bother you," he said. "I'm all right now. I wouldn't do anything to upset you on your first morning"

Ivan grinned, relieved at the news.

"I'm glad to hear it," he told Dennis.

"Worries too much, does Ron," Dennis said, reflectively. "Never takes his eyes off me. It's like living in a bleeding goldfish bowl."

Ivan looked more closely at Dennis. He was a good-looking young man, of about Ivan's age. He seemed fairly cheerful, which made Ivan wonder why he had ever tried to kill himself. Dennis noticed his expression, and grinned.

"I suppose you'd like to know why I did it?" he asked.

Ivan felt a little embarrassed.

"I'm sorry. I hadn't meant to stare."

"That's all right. You're only wondering the same things that my family wondered. They couldn't understand it, either." Dennis's expression suddenly changed. His eyes were red and filled with tears.

"I'm sorry…," Ivan began.

"No need to be. It's all over, now. Crying and feeling sorry for myself won't mend the past. That's what I've learnt since I came here."

He walked away quickly and went back to the basin. Ron came back up the stairs, carrying a packet of razor blades. Ivan, still feeling uncomfortable, told him what Dennis had said.

Ron reassured him, speaking in a low voice, not to be overheard by the patients.

"Don't worry about it. He's got to learn to live with the situation."

"What happened to him?" Ivan asked.

"His girlfriend died. She had a congenital heart condition. Dennis knew that she had to take things easy, but he insisted on taking her to a football match. She got rather excited and collapsed. He felt guilty about it, blaming himself for her death, although the doctors told him that it could have happened at any time. Three weeks after the funeral, he jumped into the river. A policeman saw him go in and rescued him. They bought him here from Casualty (nowadays called "Accident and Emergency" or "A&E"). All we could get out of him at first was 'Carol', he kept repeating the name over and over. The doctor prescribed E.C.T. for him; that's electrical treatment. It's used to treat depression. He's much better now, but he still has to live with the bad memories. Whether or not he ultimately becomes able to re-join the human race and emerge from his protracted state of mourning is as much up to Dennis as it is to us … more so, in fact."

Ivan looked thoughtful. This was an aspect of nursing that he realised he had not considered, nor had anyone warned him about it. He felt completely inadequate. How could he, or anyone else, help Dennis and others like him to come to terms with the situation. Although he was fairly resilient, Ivan wondered how he might have reacted, had he found himself in Dennis's position.

"Look," Ron said, noticing his expression. "It won't help him if you get yourself involved with his problems. We have to help him to readjust. Just talk to him about everyday things, and you'll find that he'll be OK. As for the rest of it, he'll just have to work that out in his own way."

He handed the packet of razor blades to Ivan. "Put one in Dennis's razor and watch while he shaves. When he's finished, take it out, wash it, and use it for one of the others. They should get fifteen shaves out of each blade, so I'll leave you a couple more."

Ivan looked surprised.

"Fifteen shaves? I don't get as many as that. Can't they have a new blade each time?"

Ron looked despairingly.

"I can see that you have a lot to learn. Where do you think we are, Butlins? We get supplied with a dozen blades every Thursday and they have to last us for a week. The stores would go bloody spare if we asked for any more than that. This is public money that we're spending, you know!" He walked away, leaving Ivan in charge, with a stern warning not to let any of the blades out of his sight.

"Trusting soul, ain't he?" said Dennis, as Ivan loaded his razor. "Mind you, I wouldn't know about some of these other blokes, so I should do as he says."

After Ron's departure, Ivan again began to feel like a goldfish which had jumped from its bowl to lie flapping on the carpet under the sideboard. Two days ago, he had been doing a perfectly ordinary job in a factory. Two months earlier than that, he had never in his wildest dreams thought, that one day he would be responsible for the safety and well-being of a group of psychiatric patients. He watched the men shaving with what he thought was an appropriate level of diligence, being particularly observant whenever he put a blade into a razor.

"Oy!" Dennis grinned.

"What's up?" asked Ivan.

"Your eyes are burning bleeding great holes in my back."

"Sorry. I didn't mean to stare," Ivan said, embarrassed.

"That's all right. mate, you'll pick it up."

"Pick what up?"

"The art of tactful observation!" Dennis grinned again, amused at Ivan's discomfiture.

Ivan thought about what Ron had said. He was right. There was a lot to learn!

Ron came back a few minutes later, to Ivan's vast relief. They escorted the patients to the dining room for breakfast. It was here that Ivan had his first sight of the female patients, and the nurses who were in charge of them. The reception hospital was built in the shape of a large 'E'. The centre wing housed the kitchen, the dining room, the E.C.T. suite and sundry offices. The living accommodation for the patients formed the ends of the 'E'. The females occupied one end, and the males the other. The dining room was the only room shared by both sexes. Even here, the women sat at the opposite end to the men.

A male and a female nurse were working behind the counter of the servery, handing out plates of food to their respective patients, who queued from opposite ends of this cafeteria type counter. Ivan noticed that there was little or no conversation taking place between the males and females. He remarked on this to Ron.

"We don't encourage contact," Ron said, gravely. "We have enough problems, without asking for more." Ivan was about to question Ron's meaning, but the Staff Nurse's expression warned him off.

Ron handed the care of this particular group of patients over to Pete, who had just joined them in the room. He then took Ivan back along the corridor to the observation dormitory. He explained that this was where the newly admitted or more disturbed patients were cared for, where they could be closely observed until their mental state and behaviour could be thoroughly assessed.

The dormitory was an 'L' shaped room, the shorter wall of which consisted of a row of French windows which led out onto a veranda. The beds were placed with their heads to the opposite wall of the room. Ron told Ivan to move the bed table from the foot of each bed further along towards the head, to allow breakfast to be served to the beds' occupants. One patient, who looked very morose, had a vase of flowers on his bed table. Ivan lifted the vase, which slipped from his grasp, casting the vase, flowers and water into the bed with the unfortunate patient. Ron and another nurse changed the now saturated bed linen whilst

Ivan looked on, horrified by the effects of his clumsiness.

The patient, seeing Ivan's predicament, beckoned him over.

"Never mind mate," he said. "Worse things happen at sea." This was twice in the past hour that Ivan had been reassured by a patient. Somehow, he couldn't help feeling that the boot was quite definitely on the wrong foot.

The serving of breakfast passed without further noteworthy event. Dishes were cleared away, and the ward was tidied. Ivan was just wondering what he should do next when Bob Bracewell appeared in the doorway.

"Come with me, young man," he beckoned to Ivan. "I want a few words with you."

Ivan followed, not without some trepidation.

They arrived in the office. "Sit down, son," Bob said, taking his own seat behind the desk.

To Ivan's surprise, he offered a cigarette. Ivan politely declined and sat back to listen to the Charge Nurse.

Bob explained, in a friendlier tone, exactly what Ivan's duties would comprise. He asked where Ivan's personal interests lay and was also interested in the boy's first reactions to psychiatric nursing. By the end of the conversation, Ivan found that he had developed a considerable regard for Bracewell. He was impressed by the Charge

Nurse's obvious enthusiasm for his profession, and his insistence on high standards of care for his patients. The man projected an aura of dedication, which had none of the self-righteous air of those who claimed this quality in other fields of work. It was almost as though Bracewell was afraid to admit to being, in fact, a man who had spent most of his adult life caring for those who were less fortunate than the majority.

The weeks passed by, and Ivan gradually eased into his new role in life. He occasionally reflected on how far away the factory and his former lifestyle now seemed. After only a few weeks, he felt as though he had always been a nurse. Whatever 'bug' of enthusiasm infested Bob Bracewell and the other staff had now bitten Ivan. Those bugs leave permanent teeth marks.

After two months, Ivan had come to realise that many of Ron's anxieties about the untrustworthy nature of the patients were ill founded, although he recognised the need for caution. Dennis was eventually discharged from the hospital, having quite recovered his former cheery nature.

CHAPTER FOUR

Ivan entered his training in October of that year, at the commencement of a course which was to occupy him for the next three years. The final examination seemed to be a long way ahead, and over the six weeks of the Preliminary Training School, he was given a wide view of the curriculum which he was to study. The PTS, as this preliminary six weeks were referred to, was spent almost entirely in the training school, where the student's received lectures and joined in on discussions with their tutors on the various subjects which were elementary to their training. This was also time for familiarising themselves with the geography of the hospital, and they visited each of the wards with Ted Jones, the principal tutor.

This was Ivan's first insight into the long stay wards, where many of the patients had lived for more than twenty years, and he began to wonder for the first time in months, whether he had chosen the right career. These people were very different to the patients who Ivan had known in the admission ward.

Ted Jones told them that many of the patients suffered from schizophrenia, one of the most serious forms of mental illness. This often led to bizarre behaviour, and occasionally, violence. These untoward factors were controlled in part by medication, but Ted and the staff of the wards laid great importance on the skill of the nursing staff in knowing all that there was to know about those who were in their care, and in recognising changes in behaviour which may indicate a change in the patients' mental state.

At the end of the six weeks, Ivan was once more allocated to Male Reception, and he was pleased to find that he was to work on Bob Bracewell's shift again. Vic Murdoch and Jock McCracken, two of Ivan's newly found friends from the school, went there with him.

Drawing on the knowledge gained from their lectures, the students found that they were now able to recognise some of the illnesses which beset their patients. Bob adopted an attitude of amused tolerance to the smug assurance which these, and every generation of first year students who preceded them, had developed. There were to be many occasions when he would take sadistic pleasure in destroying their illusions with a few well-chosen facts that had somehow escaped their observation.

They'll learn, he would think to himself, then he would smile as he remembered the days when he too thought of himself as a saviour of the profession.

Vic Murdoch was a stockily built, dark haired individual who had recently completed his National Service in the RAF. Ivan, who still harboured a few lingering doubts about whether he should have joined the ranks of the 'Brylcreem Boys', was discussing the subject with Vic over their breakfast break one morning. Jock entered the dining room and joined them at the table.

"Oh yes!" said Vic, leaning back in his chair with an air of authority. "You should have taken the opportunity whilst it was yours. It's a grand life in the air force."

"Oh aye, and I suppose that you made air vice-marshal, did you?" Jock chided him, in his broad Aberdonian accent.

Vic shot him a contemptuous look. "What do you know about it?" he asked the balding Scot.

"Not much. I only did fifteen years as a regular, and if you ask me, Ivan, you did the right thing in coming here instead."

Ivan's mischievous sense of humour latched into gear, as he saw an opportunity for a little light entertainment at his friends' expense.

He turned to Jock with a serious expression. "I didn't realise that you'd been a regular, Jock," he said, almost with reverence. "Tell me, was it easy to gain a promotion?"

Jock looked a little wary as he considered his answer.

"Aye, well it's there if you're prepared to work for it. What rank did you get to Vic?

"AC2. They wanted me to stay in at the end of my 'National,' — promised me three stripes, but I decided enough was enough." He nonchalantly flicked a crumb from his blue serge uniform jacket.

"Hm!" Jock reflected. "I see! And I suppose that they were distressed when you decided to leave, were they?" He winked at Ivan, unseen by Vic.

"They were, really, but I was firm with them." Vic began to look a little uneasy.

"You know," said Jock, thoughtfully. "It's a very small world. I was in the pay section, and the last discharge dossier that I processed before I left was on a Victor Murdoch. He would have been about your age. The reason that it sticks in my mind is that this fellow came out as an A.C.2, and his C.O. reported on his discharge papers that he wouldn't have been able to support this particular airman's application for regular service. You never know Vic, he might have been a relative of yours."

Vic gave Jock a look that would have stopped a clock. He stormed out of the dining room, leaving the two former companions and 'so called' friends, falling about laughing.

"Did you really work on his papers?" Ivan asked Jock.

"No!" Jock said, derisively. "I was steward in the officer's mess at RAF Lossiemouth when I finished. It was just what you might call an educated guess!"

They both curled up laughing again as they followed the affronted Vic back to the ward.

Vic was still simmering a little when Bob Bracewell called all the students into his office later in the morning. It was Bob's practice to take advantage of every opportunity to teach his students, and this was to be one of his 'question and answer' sessions.

"What illness do you think Mr Brown is suffering from?" he asked Ivan.

"I would have thought that it may be a manic-depressive episode," Ivan answered, eruditely.

"Oh yes, and what leads Dr Reader to that diagnosis?" asked Bob, the master of sarcastic humour.

"Well, when I spoke to Mr Brown just before breakfast, he seemed quite cheerful. About half an hour ago though, I saw him sitting in the dining room with tears running down his face. That's mood swinging, isn't it, or it could be emotional ambivalence?"

Ivan looked uncertainly at the Charge Nurse, who smiled faintly.

"What do you think?" he asked Vic.

Vic adopted the same attitude that he had taken with Ivan earlier, the look of the man who knows all the answers.

"I agree with Ivan's theory. It seems quite clear that Mr Brown's mood varies with the hour."

"And you?" Bob asked, turning to Jock.

"Aye, well it might be right, but there again it may not," answered the Scot, at his canniest.

"So much for the poly-syllabic crap that you've all been spouting since you finished the PTS," Bob barked, angrily. "How many times have I told you to read the patient's notes? See what the doctor has written down. Talk to the patient and make your own observations before you jump to any conclusions."

The Charge Nurse's expression softened a little.

"Now I'll put you straight," he said, more amiably. "Mr Brown was suffering from an intense grief reaction. His wife died six months ago, and he couldn't cope at home without her. We've tried to teach him how to manage his domestic chores in the Occupational Therapy Department, but when a man gets into his seventies, he doesn't learn new things very quickly. We didn't hold out much hope for him until yesterday. It was beginning to look as though he would need some kind of institutional care for the rest of his life. But then, yesterday, he had a letter from his widowed sister in Manchester. She wants him to go and live there. We told the doctor, and he told Mr Brown that he could go, and that we would put him on the train for Manchester if he could arrange for the sister to meet him at the other end. That's why the old boy was so cheerful this morning."

"But why was he crying later?" Ivan asked, puzzled.

The charge nurse grinned. "I told you that we've been trying to teach him to cook. For the last three weeks, he's been helping the chef in the main kitchen. When you saw him, he'd just finished peeling the onions for lunch!"

The students looked embarrassed, then Vic started to laugh, being rapidly joined by the other three.

"Oh man!" Vic spluttered, "so much for my diagnostic skills!"

Bob smiled. He could remember similar mistakes in his early days.

The students were allocated to each ward for fourteen weeks. At the end of each of these periods, they all moved to another type of experience, covering each ward twice during their three years of training. Ivan had only worked on Male Reception to date, and it was with some trepidation that he went to the notice board outside Mr Hunting's office, to see where he had been posted for his next fourteen weeks.

'Male Ten. 'A' shift' was the message typed against his name. This information meant little to him, as Male Ten was the one ward which he had not yet visited. It was without particular emotion, that he told Bob Bracewell where he was to be moved to. Bob's reaction amazed him. The Charge Nurse smiled a little, then he grinned broadly.

"Where did you say?" he asked the hapless Ivan, as Ron came into the office.

"Male Ten, 'A' shift," Ivan answered, innocently.

"Oh, my gawd!" Ron exclaimed. He looked at Bob, and they both burst into laughter.

"Oh, bloody hell! He'll bloody eat you!" Bob gurgled. "You're just the type that he dislikes the most."

"Who is?" Ivan asked, alarmed. "What do you mean?"

"Hoo! Hoo! Ha! Hee! Hee!" Bob guffawed. "Never mind kid, it's only for three months. Hee! Hee! Hee! Hah! Hah!"

Ivan began to feel a little panic stricken.

"What's he laughing at?" he asked Ron, but the Staff Nurse was himself too convulsed in laughter to answer.

Being unable to gain an explanation for this extraordinary behaviour by his seniors, Ivan left off duty that day somewhat perplexed.

He joined some second-year students at the lunch table.

"I'm going to Male Ten, on the 'A' shift," he announced, wondering if the news would produce a similar reaction in these specimens. It did! They roared with laughter, Ivan's discomfiture was growing by the minute, particularly when his attempts to elucidate who 'he' was bought forth a similar ambiguity to that which Bob and Ron had earlier fallen into. As he was now 'living in', he withdrew to his room for the afternoon to ponder upon these strange happenings.

As a young lady by the name of Alice had once observed, the situation became curiouser and curiouser when Ivan arrived on duty the following morning. Whoever he tried to pin down for an answer to his question, merely evaded the issue, or were so overcome by mirth that Ivan decided not to try to make any sense out of them. Whilst the aforementioned female was not a usual occupant of his thoughts, Ivan began to feel a certain affinity with her bewilderment. Bob played the part of the Cheshire cat, with Ron adopting the haste to get away from one of Alice's earlier acquaintances, the White Rabbit. Whenever our hero raised the question of a certain ward and more particularly the 'A' shift on that ward, Ron dashed off on some urgent errand of mercy, all the while having great difficulty in stifling a disquieting tendency to burst into hysterical laughter all over again.

Bob called Ivan into the office in mid-morning, his ostensible reason for doing so being to discuss Ivan's 'end of term' report. Whilst gratified by the Charge Nurse's assessment of his performance, Ivan still felt a little 'needled' by Bob's ill-disguised amusement at the obvious anxiety that his remarks the day before had produced in the lad.

"Look!" said Ivan, with more gravity than Bob felt the situation demanded. "Who's this bloke on Male Ten that you will say will eat me?"

Bob looked at the lad sitting on the other side of the desk. Enough was enough, he thought. After all, Ivan wasn't a bad kid, and it was time to end his agony. The joke had become a trifle thin. "All right," he said. "I'll put you out of your misery!"

"I wish you would," Ivan said irritably. "Who is he then?"

"Joe Joiner," said Bob. "The 'daddy' of all the Charge Nurses. If you thought I was a hard case at first, wait until you meet Joe!"

He went on to describe Mr Joiner's less pleasant attributes in lurid detail, again referring to his propensity for eating students for breakfast. Whilst Ivan realised that Bob was speaking metaphorically, and that he was still probably 'laying it on thick', he found Mr Joiner's dietary habits not to be to his own liking. After all, no one enjoys being part of the kedgeree, even metaphorically.

Fortunately, Bob detected Ivan's anxiety, and deciding enough was enough, he spoke reassuringly.

"You'll get on with Joe all right, provided that you remember one or two points. There are two things that really annoy him — lateness and untidiness. Whatever else you may do, don't let him catch you coming in late, or give him the opportunity to criticise your appearance. They're just the sort of things that will bring him down on you like a ton of bricks."

Ivan thanked Bob for his advice and went on his way, not exactly rejoicing. He would have felt more reassured by Bob's words, had not the latter dismally failed to stop himself from periodically grinning from ear to ear every time that he looked at the hapless lad in the eye. With a strong sense of foreboding, Ivan walked out of the familiar surroundings of the Male Reception, bravely setting his sails in the teeth of the winds of fate.

CHAPTER FIVE

Ivan arrived on Male Ten at ten minutes to seven on the Sunday morning, with Bob Bracewell's words still ringing in his ears. Immaculate in his clean white coat and highly polished shoes, he mentally prepared himself for his first meeting with the now infamous Mr Joiner.

As he entered the ward dormitory, some of the patients were getting up. Ivan noticed that as each one did so, he made his own bed, folded his pyjamas and stowed them away under the pillows. Most were dressing in the herringbone 'Derby Grey' suits that Ivan had seen issued to the few patients on Male Reception who could not provide their own clothing. Black buckled shoes seemed to be the standard type of footwear.

The night nurse came into the dormitory, yawning the yawn of one who had just emerged from the seemingly interminable hours of darkness. Ivan recognised him as one of the third-year students who was about to sit his 'finals'.

"Hello," said the nocturnal one. "Is this your first day up here?"

Ivan answered in the affirmative. "Is Mr Joiner here yet?" he asked.

"No, not yet. Have you met him?" he smiled faintly.

"Not yet, but I've heard about him."

"What have you heard then?"

"Well, nothing specific," Ivan said warily. "I gather he is something of a character?"

The night nurse looked at Ivan and grinned. "He's all of that all right, and more besides." Controlling an obvious desire to burst into laughter, he bade Ivan 'good morning' and left the ward.

Ivan now felt as though he was standing in the middle of a crowded street in his birthday suit, seeing no familiar face or object in the immediate environment to help him overcome his ordeal. A patient came over towards him, holding out his hand in greeting.

"I'm Harry," he said. "Are you the new attendant?"

Ivan was a little taken aback by Harry's use of the title 'attendant' but he passed no comment.

"I'm Ivan Reader," he said returning Harry's handshake.

"Ah! Well, Mr Joiner won't be here yet Mister, it's Sunday." Harry sounded a little mysterious, speaking in the broad tones of the northern part of the county.

"What's special about Sunday?" Ivan asked.

"Mr Joiner says it's the day of rest. He won't give you much rest though! Tarrah!"

Harry went about his business, leaving Ivan in a more highly charged state of nervousness than before. Noticing his somewhat vacuous expression, Harry came back to him.

"Look, you straighten the beds up after the lads have made them, and I'll show you how Mr Joiner likes them done."

So saying, he produced, from a cupboard, a wooden frame, which he placed across the gap between the two beds. Ivan now realised that this gadget was designed to space the beds a uniform distance apart, and he watched fascinated as Harry pulled the creases out of the counterpane and folded the rear edges of the pillowcases underneath, tightening the fabric across the pillow. Harry explained that Mr Joiner had made the ingenious looking frame, and that he insisted upon its use. At a quarter past seven, the door at the bottom end of the dormitory suddenly opened. This produced an electrifying effect on the patients, sending them scuttling in all directions.

"Good morning, Mr Joiner," Harry said.

A snarl emanated from the recently opened door to Ivan's rear. Turning, Ivan caught his first sight of the man who he had heard so much, and yet knew so little, about.

The apparition in the doorway bore no resemblance at all to the mental image of Joiner which had been forming in Ivan's mind. Ivan had imagined a tall, guardsman like figure, with a neatly clipped moustache and a steely eye. Instead, there stood a tubby little man of some five foot six. His bald head seemed the more so for the fringe of black, uncombed hair. He wore neither collar nor tie, and his blue serge uniform waistcoat hung unbuttoned under his jacket, revealing a pair of old fashioned 'button on' braces. The craggy, weather-beaten face bore what Ivan interpreted as a look of threatened homicide. His nose was bent, like a bust of Julius Caesar that Ivan had seen in a museum.

"Good morning, Mr Joiner," Ivan ventured, a little hoarsely

"Umph!" the Charge Nurse grunted. And walked straight past Ivan, through the day room and into the ward office.

"He's never very talkative at this time of day, Mister," Harry said.

Ivan wondered whether he should follow Joiner into the office, but his guardian angel, who Ivan was about to dismiss for dereliction of duty, made him think better of it. Not knowing what else to do, Ivan carried on with the task of straightening the beds.

Subsequent events revealed this to be sound policy on our hero's part, as Harry testified when he appeared a few minutes later, bearing with him a cup of tea.

"You're OK Mister, he's sent you this down." He handed the tea to the mystified Ivan. Once more, Harry provided the explanation. "That means he's in a good mood. Take my advice. If any morning he doesn't send one down, keep out of his way until about half past ten!"

Once more, Ivan had the uncomfortable feeling that most of the reassuring that had been going on had been a stream of one-way traffic from Harry to him.

Ivan thanked Harry for the tea and surveyed the results of his efforts in the dormitory as he drank it. He had, he felt, reason to be proud of his work. The beds stood in perfectly straight lines, parallel to the floorboards. They were all spaced an even distance apart, the result of his diligent application of the wooden frame, bearing no signs of creases in either pillow or counterpane.

As he finished the tea, he looked down the length of the day room, which stretched from the doorway. One of the patients had laid the tables for breakfast, and another had just wheeled an electrically heated food trolley, containing the breakfast, into the ward.

The patients all stood with their backs to the wall. They were obviously awaiting permission from Joiner to be seated, with the exception of one old chap who walked with the aid of two sticks. Hearing the clatter of metal containers being unloaded from the trolley in the scullery, Ivan went to help. He picked up a tin of boiled tomatoes and placed it alongside the tray of bacon which Joiner had put on a large tea trolley.

"What the bloody 'ell are yow doing?" Joiner bellowed, in a broad black country accent.

"Did I tell yow to bloody well do anything?"

"Well, well, er no Mr Joiner," Ivan stammered.

"Well bugger off back in the dormitory then, until I send for yow," he roared.

Ivan 'buggered off back' as bidden, wondering what he had done wrong.

"Ah'll be commin' down to look at them bloody beds soon," Joiner yelled at Ivan's retreating back.

"Yow mek sure the buggers is raight!"

Ivan made sure the 'buggers were raight' several times over when Harry eventually rejoined him.

"Mr Joiner wants to see you," Harry said. "He's in the scullery."

With more than a little trepidation, Ivan re-entered the scullery. Two patients were washing up the breakfast dishes.

"Com' in 'ere yowth," shouted Joiner from the small larder room at the rear.

He was sitting at a small table, reading the morning paper and smoking a Woodbine. A steaming plate of bacon and tomatoes lay in the place opposite Joiner, a large mug of tea at its side.

"Sit yow down an' get your breakfast," Joiner said to Ivan's amusement.

"Er, aren't you having any Mr Joiner?" Ivan asked, nervously.

"Ulcer!" he grated, returning to his paper.

Ivan ate in silence. As he finished, he noticed that Joiner had put down his paper, and had obviously been studying the lad for some time. Joiner smiled.

"Ah'm plaised ter say that yer can ate!" he said. "Yow need some snap in yer in this job."

"Er, yes, very nice, thank you," Ivan replied, hesitantly.

"Aahr, that's alraight. Now! I'll tell yer a thing or tow. I'm Joe Joiner, and yow mun call may Joe as long as Mr Hunting ai' around. If 'im or any bugger else is in the ward, its Mr Joiner, see?"

"Yes, I see."

"Aahr. Good! Now, ah expect as yow'll 'ave bin workin' wi' that Bob Bracewell, over there, an' ay'll 'ave towd yow that as yow're a student, yow should ask questions an' learn. Well lad, ah'm the gaffer 'ere, an' ah like things done a bit different. If ah tells yow to do somethin', yow does it, an' don't ask any stupid bloody questions. If ah wants yow to know owt, ah'll tell yer, see? Other than that, just mind yer own business, an' yow an' may'll get on all raight."

Ivan, surprised by the man's change of mood, found that he was beginning to warm to this earthy character.

"Yes, I see Mr. Joiner," he said.

"Aahr. Well, yow remember that then kid, an' yow'll find it'll pay yer. Now, ah expect you'll be thinkin' as ah'm a rum owd bugger, an' p'raps I am; but ah'm tow bloody owd ter start changin' now. Yow do raight bar may, an' yow'll be all raight, ah'll see ter that. Yow'll learn a bit an' all. Bracewell don't bloody know it all!"

Ivan now realised that his first impression of Joe had been quite wrong. He could now see what had caused the hilarity amongst the staff on Male Reception, as no amount of preparation by Bob Bracewell would really have helped. The thought of generations of students falling foul of Joe on their first meeting with him caused Ivan some little amusement. Amongst their ranks would, of course, have been Bob Bracewell, Ron Mount and everyone else who had worked with him over the last thirty years. They knew that Ivan's first morning with Joe was a gauntlet that just had to be run.

Joe's own view of the matter was that these lads would have far rougher rides ahead of them in the course or their careers, and that if they wilted in the glare of his fiery personality, they would probably not stay the course.

"Kill or cure," could have been his motto, but only with reference to the staff.

The first week of Ivan's apprenticeship under this master of his craft went by without further notable incident, except that Ivan heard Joe use a few words of invective that he previously hadn't realised were part of the English language. He was to find that Joe was an expert in the art of 'cussing' with a command of the language and a vocabulary that would have caused Shakespeare to catch his breath in admiration.

As previously reported in these columns, Ivan was blessed with a powerful sense of humour, and Joe's propensity for the profane provided him with endless fun. By the end of his first week on the ward, he had recognised that Joe was, in his own way, a poet, although he didn't know whether the Charge Nurse's particular style of prose would have cut much ice with Patience Strong. He had to wait until the Wednesday of the following week, however, before he heard Joe produce what could only be described as his masterpiece.

Joe Joiner was a man of many parts, and one of these parts was his role of racing tipster to the rest of the staff of the Meadows. At five o'clock each evening, he would switch on the ward radio and check the fortunes of his various selections. Absolute silence was called for during these interludes, and it was woe betide anyone who dared to interrupt the master at his studies. The lesson had been well learnt by the patients, and they studiously avoided the incurrence of Joe's wrath at these times. Ivan was therefore a little surprised when halfway through this particular set of results, Joe suddenly launched into a soliloquy that would have ranked equal with Hamlet's efforts on the battlements of Elsinore, or Churchill's 'never in the field, etcetera', had it been recorded for posterity.

Ivan had to admit that Joe's prosaic progressions on this occasion were truly artistic. He strung together words with the virtuosity of Menhuin, the eloquence of Aneurin Bevan, and the flourish of Rembrandt. At the end of the recital, Ivan plucked up courage to enquire as to what had stirred the muse in Joe's breast on this occasion. The aforementioned breast swelled and heaved with indignance and scorn as Joe explained the cause of his anguish.

Joe's philosophy of racing tipsterism was based on a simple, self-imposed rule of life. This simple tenet was that he never backed a horse himself that he had 'given' to anyone else. The principle had stood him in good stead over the years, but this time, the trick had backfired on its originator. He had intended to back 'Eskimo Nell' in the three-thirty at Kempton, but in an unguarded moment, he had recommended the nag to a drinking acquaintance who had fallen upon hard times. In deference to the above policy, Joe had transferred both his affections and his stake money to 'Happy Harry' in the same race. Happy Harry had led throughout, with Eskimo Nell a close second. Joe had thought his faith in his own methods had been completely vindicated, but a steward's enquiry had awarded the race to Eskimo Nell, who carried odds of a 100 to one. Like the man said, true art is oft born of human anguish!

Every Wednesday evening, whichever shift of a 'Charge Nurse and a lad' were on duty, it was Bingo at seven p.m. There was an old Oxo tin, which was kept under lock and key in the office, and in it were many threepenny pieces, plus a couple of plastic money bags containing bank notes.

The Charge Nurse would call the numbers, and the Student Nurse would check the card of whoever called 'House' or 'Here' or 'ER' (Here

You Are!) at the end of every game. The stakes were always threepence per card — win a shilling!

Over the twelve weeks of Ivan's 'tenancy' on Male Ten, he noticed the amount of cash in the tin mounting up, but Joe's early instruction about asking questions prevented him from doing just that!

With the exception of his racing tips, Ivan was to see Joe in a far more favourable light over the next few weeks. Although he had initially formed the impression that Joe was not as professionally orientated as Bob Bracewell, the fact was that Joe's vast experience of nursing the mentally ill had given him an expertise that was second to none. Not one small item of information concerning the wellbeing of his patients ever escaped his attention, and Ivan often felt humbled by the man's skill in this and many other directions. Only once did Ivan have cause to doubt Joe's infallibility, and that concerned Ivan's duty rota.

One Friday, Joe said, "You'd better go up to the office — Harold Marston wants a word with you."

"What about?" Ivan asked.

"You'll see. Go on — he's waiting for you!"

'The Office' that Joe had referred to was next to Mr Hunting's office. There was an adjoining door. It was where the Assistant Chief Male Nurses would be based, working on duty and holiday rotas, answering the phones, and generally taking charge of the male side of the hospital for that particular shift. Assistant Chief was the next rank up from Charge Nurse.

Ivan knocked on the door with a little trepidation. Staff were normally only summoned to the office if they had transgressed in some way, but Ivan couldn't think of anything he had done wrong!

After calling Ivan in, Mr Marston said, "Ah — Ivan! Thanks for coming up. I wondered if you might be prepared to help us out. I know you are off next weekend, (the duty rota at that time was such that the nurses' day off progressed a day forward each week, resulting in a weekend off every seven weeks) but we wondered if you would mind doing a double shift next Saturday, then taking Saturday, Sunday and Monday off the following week?"

After a little thought, Ivan said, "No, that would be fine for me Mr Marston."

"Good lad! Shut the door as you go out, please!"

Ivan walked back to the ward a little mystified.

"Well?" Joe asked.

Ivan explained what Mr Marston had asked.

"That's OK then. Don't be late in the mornin'."

It was now the end of the morning shift — two-fifteen p.m. so Ivan went to his room, after lunch in the dining room.

The following morning — Saturday — he walked up the stairs into the dormitory as usual.

He was surprised to find that all the patients were up and dressed, washed and shaved, and the breakfast had clearly already been served and cleared away. His opposite number, Gordon, from the 'B' shift followed him in.

"What's going on? He asked Ivan.

"I dunno mate," Ivan replied.

Then both Charge Nurses — Joe and his opposite number — Charlie — emerged from the staff room.

"Ivan!" Joe shouted. "Nip down to the car park and see if the coach has arrived!"

"What coach?" he asked.

"You'll see. Just go and look!"

Knowing better than to argue, Ivan walked down the front stairs of the ward and into the car park. Sure enough, there stood a coach with its engine ticking over. He went back to the ward and said, "Yes, it's here."

Within ten minutes, everyone — all the patients and the four staff — were on board, and the driver set off.

Ivan turned to Joe. "So, where are we going?" He grinned.

"Skegness! Now sod off and let me have a kip. Charlie and I have been in since five-thirty getting them all ready."

The sun shone all day long. A day of beer, games of darts, two very good meals, walks on the beach and fun and frolics.

As they boarded the coach at six-thirty p.m. Charlie came over to Ivan.

"Thanks for helping out, mate. You and young Gordon have done a good job."

Ivan said, "Thanks Charlie. I've enjoyed it, but why didn't Joe just ask me himself?"

Charlie smiled. "Pride, mainly! A few years ago, he did ask a couple of lads to come with him, and they let him down. He ended up doing the whole day on his own! So, he won't ask now. He leaves it to the office!"

Joe saw them chatting and came over. He also thanked Ivan and Gordon, then he smiled.

"Now you both know what we do with the Bingo money!"

On the journey back, Ivan sat next to Charlie on the coach.

"Have you noticed how the lads have come out of themselves a bit today?" Charlie asked.

Ivan said, "Yes, now you mention it, I have."

Charlie said, "Just watch them go back into their shells when we get back. Have you read Erving Goffman's book — 'Asylums'?"

Ivan said no, though he'd heard about it.

Charlie answered, "I've got a copy: I'll lend it to you."

(Erving Goffman was an American Psychologist — 1920 to 1980. He studied the effects of long-term institutional life on prisoners, mental patients and other groups who live in close proximity. He postulated that one way of coping with this was for each individual to live in a personal 'bubble', with minimal interaction with his fellows).

Ivan watched the faces change as the coach rolled through the hospital gates. Goffman and Charlie were right!

CHAPTER SIX

The first twelve months of Ivan's training passed quickly. At the end of this first year, the class reassembled in the training school for two weeks of revision prior to the intermediate examination. This was the exam which was supposed to sort out the chaff from the wheat amongst the students, although it was practically unheard of for anyone at the Meadows to fail. This excellent record was mostly due to the teaching of Ted Jones, the principal tutor.

Along with his teaching role, Ted was also the students' friend, mentor, father figure and persecutor. Usually an amiable soul, he would destroy misguided confidence or complacency with a few well-chosen sentences of good natured, somewhat cynical humour.

Vic Murdoch was often the victim of Ted's wit. On one occasion, he became a little irritated by the Tutor's jibes.

"You'll damage my ego!" he retorted.

Ted raised his voice and his eyebrows. "Damage your ego? You didn't know that you had a bloody ego until I told you so!"

Those students who had formerly been Cadet Nurses were a little better equipped than the rest, in that most of them had come through Ted's 'baptism of fire' at an early stage, before commencing their formal training. The Cadets were those youngsters who were 'filling time' between leaving school and their eighteenth birthdays. As they were not allowed to actually nurse patients before the age of eighteen, they were used as general 'dogsbodies' around the various departments, attending Derfield Technical College on two days a week, in the hope they would gain the requisite 'O' levels before embarking upon their nursing training. It was those kids who Ted really 'went for' believing that he would either kill or cure them before they passed into his hands to be 'moulded' into proper nurses.

Ted's approach to the Cadets consisted largely of exposing them to various situations, and then observing their reactions. Those who laughed off the embarrassment that these situations doubtlessly created were, according to Ted, possessed of the requisite balance of humour and self-respect for the performance of their future tasks. Those who did not either left nursing for good, or eventually came round to his way of thinking.

One girl, Dawn, had been suffering under Ted's regime for a few weeks when Ivan's revision block began. A tall, pretty girl, whose tasks included making tea for all, and running errands for the Tutors.

During the afternoon tea break on the first day of block, Ted sat in his office, whilst Dawn was about her appointed task of serving tea to the students. Ivan had begun to look forward to his tea breaks, as it gave him the opportunity to watch the delightful Cadet as she went about her business. He had just managed to engage her in the preliminary stages of 'chatting up' when the wall phone in the corridor rang. Ivan went to answer it, but Ted hissed at him from the office.

"No, leave it," he commanded. "I want Dawn to answer it. You come in here and pick up the extension." His roguish grin conveyed to Ivan that it was he who had dialled the corridor phone.

"Nurse Nash, answer the phone, please," Ted bawled.

Dawn rushed down the corridor and picked up the receiver, as Ivan lifted the extension in the office.

"Hello, training school," she said.

"Could I spik to Meester Jones, plis?" asked Ted, in a fair imitation of an Indian accent.

"Who's speaking please?"

"Thees ees Dr Mahooji!"

"Just a moment, please." She ran down the corridor and tapped on the office door.

"Yep?" snapped Ted, irritably.

"Excuse me, Mr Jones, but a Dr Mahooji would like to speak to you on the other phone."

Ted was holding the office phone to his ear. He placed his hand over the mouthpiece.

"Tell him I'll ring him back," he whispered. "I'm talking to Matron at the moment."

Dawn sprinted back to her 'phone. "Hello, Dr Mahooji?"

"Hello, pliz?" said the bogus Indian 'doctor'.

"I'm sorry, but Mr Jones is on the other line. Could he call you back?"

"No pliz. I must spik with him most urgently!"

"Just a moment please." Dawn ran back to the office. "I'm sorry, but Dr Mahooji wants to speak to you urgently."

"Can't you see that I'm busy?" Ted asked angrily. "Ask him to leave a message."

Dawn did another dash along the corridor. "I'm sorry, doctor, but Mr Jones can't come to the phone. Can I take a message?"

Ted grinned evilly at Ivan and winked. "Ah yes pliz. Tell him that I have a case of Acute Paronychia that I would like the students to see. I will wait."

Dawn arrived back at the office, flushed and a little breathless. "He's got a case of acute, er, para something or other, and he would like you to take the students to see the patient."

"Ask him if it's Paratyphoid," said Ted.

Dawn trudged painfully back up the corridor. "Is it paratyphoid, Doctor?"

"No, no. Eet is Paraonchyosis."

"Paraonchyosis!"

"Yes pliz."

"It's Paraonchyosis," she announces in the office.

"Paraonchyosis?" shouted Ted. "Ask him if he thinks I've nothing better to do than cart the students about to look at ingrowing bloody toenails!"

"I can't tell him that!" said Dawn, on the verge of tears.

"Do as I say!" bawled Ted.

Dawn nervously picked up the phone. "I'm sorry, doctor," she began, "but Mr Jones is very busy at the moment. He thanks you for ringing, but says may he bring the students down later?"

"Oh, very well!" said Ted, in his best Hindustani dialect, "but Paraphrenia is quite rare. Eet would be of great value if the nurses could see it."

Dawn ran back to the office. "It's Paraphrenia, Mr Jones, not the other thing!"

"Paraphrenia, is it?" said Ted. "Well, that's different. Tell him that we will be down right away."

Dawn walked back down the corridor, exhausted. "Thank you, Doctor, Mr Jones will be down right away."

"Thank you," said the voice, and rang off.

She went back to the office yet again.

"Shall I tell the students to get ready?" she asked.

Ted looked at Ivan, and they both burst out laughing. Dawn looked perplexed. Ted, seeing her expression, laughed even more.

"Oh you!" Dawn snorted, as realisation dawned on her. She stormed back to the scullery, leaving the two men in fits of mirth.

CHAPTER SEVEN

Vic Murdoch, Jock McCracken and Ivan had become firm friends by the end of their first year of training. With the passing of the intermediate exam by all members of the trio, three months of night duty loomed ahead. It was usual for the students to go on nights at this time, and the three had been anticipating the event. No amount of preparation though, could prevent the strange mental and physical disturbances which were bought about by the inversion of Ivan's normal pattern of living. For the first two or three nights on duty, he felt physically sick, not being able to face his food, and being quite unable to catch more than two or three hours of sleep during daylight.

"You'll soon get used to it," said Vic, as they sat in the dining room over supper prior to going on duty. "I did a lot of nights in the RAF After another couple of days, you'll be so knackered that you'll sleep in the beam of a searchlight."

"Thanks!" said Ivan, disconsolately. "You're a great help."

Vic grinned sardonically and went to the servery to collect his main course. He returned with a plate of ham salad.

Jock looked at Ivan and winked as Vic tucked into his slices of ham. "Here, Vic, are you not a Catholic?"

He shot Ivan a secretive grin over Vic's shoulder.

"Yes, I am. So what?" asked Vic, suspiciously.

"Oh nothing," said Jock, trying to look unconcerned.

Vic bristled slightly, suspecting correctly that the Scot was 'extracting the Michael' again. "Why did you ask? You know that I'm R.C."

"No particular reason," Jock lied. "It's just that I was a little surprised to see you eating ham on a Friday."

"Of course! You're right," said Vic. Taking Jock's observation at face value. (Always a dangerous practice!). He rose, taking his plate back to the hatch.

"Of course," ventured Jock. "If ye belonged to a proper religion, say Presbyterianism, it wouldnae matter whit ye ate or when ye ate it!"

Vic strode away from the table, muttering.

"What did he say?" Ivan asked Jock.

"I think it was something like 'walls', he must be thinking of doing some decorating."

"I thought it sounded more like 'rowlocks'. Perhaps he's thinking of buying a boat." The pair collapsed into laughter as the somewhat ruffled Vic re-joined them, this time with fish and chips.

"It's not fair to make fun of my religion," he said, through a mouthful of battered cod. "You don't understand."

"No, you're quite right Vic," Ivan said, looking duly penitent. "It won't happen again."

"Aye, and the same goes for me," said Jock. He looked at Ivan, and the pair burst out laughing again.

"Now look here!" shouted Vic, angrily. "I won't — aaaghh!" he clutched at his throat and began to cough and splutter.

"Aach man he's choking!" said Jock, now genuinely concerned.

"Fish bone!" spluttered Vic.

"Get some water!" shouted Ivan.

"Call a doctor!" shouted Jock.

"Aaaggghhh!" shouted Vic.

"Oh my God!" screamed the waitress, as Vic turned a delicate shade of purple. She ran to the phone in the kitchen. A few seconds later, Dr Singh ran into the dining room, clutching a pair of forceps.

"What has happened pliz?" he asked, as Vic rolled on the floor in agony.

"He's swallowed a fish bone," Jock informed him.

"Oh, my goodness!" said the doctor. He took a wooden spatula from the top pocket of his white coat, and used it to press Vic's tongue down. He deftly inserted the forceps into the unfortunate Vic's gullet and extracted a large fish bone. Vic began to look better immediately. When he had sufficiently recovered, they took him to the staff sick bay, where Dr Singh carried out a more thorough examination.

"I am afraid that he will have to go to the Infirmary," Dr Singh told Jock and Ivan. "Part of the bone is still embedded in his epiglottis. He may need a small operation to remove it."

Ivan escorted Vic in the ambulance to the infirmary, and handed Vic and Dr Singh's letter over to the casualty sister.

"He'll be fine in a couple of days," Sister said, confidently. "We'll operate tonight, and you can visit him in the morning."

Ivan made his way back to the Meadows, and after telling the night superintendent what had happened, joined Jock on the ward that they were to jointly oversee for the night.

"What time's visiting down there?" Jock asked over breakfast the following morning.

"Not until eleven o'clock," Ivan replied.

"Not much point in going to bed until we've been, then. If I go to sleep now, I'll never wake up in time." He yawned expansively, as if in illustration of his point.

Ivan nodded, in silent confirmation of Jock's observation. "Why don't we go into town, have a look round the shops, and buy him some grapes or something. With any luck, we should have time for a quick pint or two before we go to the hospital."

"Good idea," said Jock.

That was the intention, at least. As many readers will know, however, time tends to pass rather rapidly when two chaps go into a pub for a quick drink, particularly when the quick drink is followed by three or four slower ones. It was just such a trick of relativity that brought Vic's friends to his bedside five minutes before visiting time ended, smelling strongly of beer and carrying a rather squashed bunch of grapes.

"Thanks lads, I really appreciate this," said Vic, his expression somehow belying his words.

"You know, Jock," Ivan said, as they walked out of the ward. "I don't somehow think that he was all that pleased to see us."

"Ach well," said Jock. "There's no pleasing some people."

Vic made a full recovery within a few days and was soon back on duty. Ivan found that the Student Nurses on night duty were called upon to accept much more responsibility than was ever expected of them by day. In theory, the Night Superintendent or night Charge Nurse were in charge, but the fact was that the students would either be alone on a ward, or in charge of a Nursing Assistant, with occasional visits from Wally Brown, the 'Super' or the Charge Nurse.

It was with slight trepidation that Ivan took over the reins of Male Reception for the first time from Bob Bracewell. He knew that the patients would all be new arrivals since he had last worked there by day, but Bob put him at ease by giving him a full breakdown of each one's case, along with a comprehensive list of points to watch.

"Don't forget, kid, if you're in any doubt, ring Wally," Ivan thanked him and returned to the observation dormitory as Bob left by the main door. Ivan's partner for the night was to be Alf Farmer, an old sweat who had worked nights at the Meadows for years. Alf had been a medical orderly in the R.A.M.C. during the war, and he had been at the Meadows ever since his 'demob' in 1946. The financial burden of a wife and two children had precluded Alf from living on the pitifully small wage of a Student Nurse, thus preventing him from taking formal training. What he lacked in education though, was supplanted by his now considerable experience, and Ivan was comforted by his presence. A good Nursing

Assistant could be invaluable to a raw student in this type of situation.

The last patient 'turned in' at ten-thirty, and Alf set out the 'nursing station' for the night. He placed an office lamp on a small, circular coffee table, casting a large enough pool of light to enable himself and Ivan to see without disturbing the patients. He pulled two fairly comfortable armchairs up to the table, then made a pot of tea.

"I've had a look upstairs, the lads are all asleep," he whispered, in his broad Yorkshire accent. "We should have a quiet night, with any luck."

The two sat down at the table and conversed in whispers as they drank their tea. The sound of the patients' rhythmical breathing, along with snores. whistles, grunts and other sounds of slumber began to exert a soporific effect on Ivan, found some difficulty in preventing his own leaden eyelids from drooping. His eyes had just closed when Alf tapped his arm, jerking him awake.

"Wake up, youth! Alf said. "Wally'll be 'ere soon. Once he's gone, we can take it in turns to grab forty winks if all's quiet."

Ivan stirred in his chair and with a seemingly colossal effort, sat up. Heaving himself to his feet, he crossed to the nearby wash basin and rinsed his face in cold water.

"I'll never get used to this bloody night duty!" he whispered.

Alf grinned. "The first ten years are the worst. I have trouble sleeping on my nights off, but I could sleep all day. If I have a couple of weeks holiday, I've just about got back to normal by the time that I'm due to come back to work. Still, I've only got five more years to do, then I can retire." He looked pleased at the prospect.

"Are you looking forward to retirement?" Ivan asked.

"Too bloody true mate. It can't come quickly enough. You'll see, this job's not so bad in some respects, but it's an uphill finish."

Ivan reflected on Alf's words. Joe Joiner had passed a similar remark to him a few months earlier.

Alf stood up.

"I'll go and have another quick look around upstairs." He walked towards the doorway. As he did so, an elderly man rose from one of the beds and made for the toilet. "Night Bill," whispered Alf.

"Night Alf," Bill replied.

Alf returned about ten minutes later. "Has Bill come out of the khazi yet?" he asked.

Ivan looked a little perturbed. "No, he hasn't. Do you think that we should go and check?"

"Might not be a bad idea. Come on, we'll look in on him." Alf opened the door to the toilet, and peered inside. A pair of feet swung gently in front of them. "Bugger! He's hung his bloody self!" Alf exclaimed. "Quick! Grab his legs and take his weight."

Ivan did as Alf had said, his heart pounding with fear. Alf climbed onto the toilet seat and untied the pyjama cord, which Bill had evidently tied to the transverse pipe before noosing the other end round his neck. As the strain came off the cord, the patient's body sagged, causing Ivan to lose his balance. He fell to the ground, with Bill's weight on top of him. Frantically, he clawed his way out from under the body and regained his feet. He looked down at Bill's face, and felt revulsion at the sight. The face was dark blue to black, the eyes bulged out of their sockets, and the swollen tongue lolled out the side of his mouth.

"Get the oxygen!" Alf commanded. Ivan was out of the dormitory and halfway back with the wheeled cylinder before he remembered that he, not Alf was supposed to be in charge. He arrived back at the toilets to find Alf administering the 'kiss of life' to Bill's recumbent form. Suddenly, the patient gagged, then coughed and spluttered. He began to breathe stertorously, drawing in great amounts of air into his lungs. His colour began to improve as Alf applied the oxygen mask to his face and turned on the life-giving gas.

"Thank God!" Alf said. "Give me a hand to get him back to bed." They carried Bill's still limp bulk back to the bed a few feet away and laid the patient on his side. His breathing was more regular now, and he began to regain consciousness. Ivan telephoned the duty doctor, who came to the ward within minutes, closely followed by Wally Brown. The doctor examined Bill thoroughly, and pronounced him to be in good shape, apart from a nasty bruise which encircled his neck.

"Bloody 'ell, that was close," Alf said, as the ward settled down again.

Ivan was trembling from head to foot as he recalled the events of the past half hour. "I'm glad you were here, Alf," he said, with sincere gratitude.

"Ah well," Alf grunted, as he opened the evening paper. "I told you that the first ten years were the worst, didn't I?"

"All the same though, I don't think I'd have coped as well as you did, had I been on my own."

Alf put down the paper. "Perhaps you should talk to Wally about it. He can tell you more than I can about the technical aspects of this kind of thing. You'll know a bit more about it the next time it happens to you though, won't you?" He grinned paternalistically at the lad.

Ivan made a point of discussing the incident with Wally Brown when the night superintendent returned later. Wally reassured him that Bill was unlikely to try the same thing again in the immediate future.

"Whilst you should still keep a tactful eye on him, I think you'll find that he'll improve steadily over the next few weeks. He's passed his crisis now, and cases such as this often progress rapidly once they've got it out of their system. You should read up on Freud's ideas on what he called catharsis. There should be some books on the subject in the school library." He left the ward, and a slightly older more pensive Ivan.

The weeks passed by without further notable events. Ivan was now seeing Dawn regularly on his nights off, and he found her increasingly occupying his thoughts during the long night shifts.

"You're in love!" said Vic, mockingly, as he tried to command his moonstruck colleague's attention over supper one night. The night staff were allowed to visit each other's wards during their supper breaks, and Ivan, Jock and Vic regularly met at those times.

"Aye, he is that!" Jock agreed. "He looks awful' like the old bull used to do at home, before we put him to the heifers."

Ivan awoke from his reverie and replied to their remarks with a couple of well-aimed spoonsful of glutinous custard which the night cook, a former merchant navy engine room attendant, had drowned the soggy sponge in. Vic was about to return his fire when the phone in the ward office rang. As Vic was in charge of this particular ward, he answered.

"Who's with you at the moment?" asked Wally Brown.

"I've got Jock and Ivan here on their supper breaks," Vic replied.

"Ah good would you and Jock mind walking over to the female nurses' home? I'll join Vic on the ward whilst you go. We've had a report of a prowler. I suppose it's only Miss Farquaharson's wishful thinking again, but we had better check." He rang off.

Jock smiled. Miss Farquaharson was a middle-aged Assistant Matron who lived in the nurses' home for over twenty years. She had become something of a standing joke amongst the male nurses on night duty, who suspected that her frequent reports of prowlers were a subtle device to lure Wally to her boudoir. Whilst Wally ridiculed the idea, he obviously wasn't taking any chances, as he usually delegated the investigation of such reports to his juniors, as he had, in fact, done on the night in question.

Having been caught for this job before, Ivan and Jock took their time in getting to the scene of the 'crime', knowing that their search would probably be fruitless. They were somewhat surprised, therefore, to discover a group of about a dozen nurses clad in dressing gowns babbling excitedly and pointing up at the roof.

"There's a man up there!" Miss Farquaharson informed them triumphantly, her previous false alarms now vindicated.

"Bloody hell, there is too," Ivan whispered to Jock.

Jock shone his powerful torch on the dormer window which was the object of so much attention from the ladies. The beam illuminated the inebriate form of Cliff Banks, a third-year student. Only now did Ivan realise that the dormer on which Cliff was so precariously perched was that of the room occupied by Janet Green, Cliff's fiancée until a few days before, when she had thrown the ring at him during one of their increasingly frequent rows in the dining room, a valued source of amusement to the other staff.

"Get him down from there at once, young man," Miss Farquaharson commanded Ivan. "He'll have a serious accident otherwise."

Ivan, who was no slouch himself when it came to reasoning, could appreciate the logical basis of Miss Farquaharson's fears. As a preliminary move, he set about dispersing the crowd of giggling, gasping, gaping females. Miss Farquaharson, being made of sterner stuff than the students, insisted on staying, to supervise events.

"Will ye come doon mon?" shouted Jock.

"Sod off, Haggis!" came the reply from the rooftop.

"Cliff! Come down before you break your stupid neck!" Ivan shouted, trying the subtle approach.

Cliff leaned over precariously. "Piss off, Reader. Mind your own bloody business." He teetered still nearer to the edge, drawing a gasp of horror from Miss F.

"He's going to fall!" she screamed, reassuringly.

Cliff was now hanging over the edge of the roof, peering invertedly into Janet's window.

"Do you bloody love me or don't you?" he roared, whilst Janet cowered within, terrified. Cliff took a large gulp from the bottle of Scotch which he had grasped by the neck throughout the interlude.

Jock turned to Miss Farquaharson. "See if you can persuade the lassie to come out here. She might be able to get the bloody fool to come down."

"Well really!" Miss Farquaharson snorted. "I'm not at all sure — Oh well! I suppose it might work." She disappeared into the home.

"Let's get the ladder," Ivan said. They ran to the builder's yard, a couple of hundred yards away, returning breathless a few minutes later.

Janet was now outside, pleading with Cliff. "Come down, darling, you'll hurt yourself."

"Much you'd bloody care," came Cliff's 'spirited' reply.

"I would, darling, I still love you," Janet sobbed.

Miss Farquaharson turned with misty eyes to the two male nurses, who stood holding the ladder, feeling as much at one with the scene above them as Custer would have done at Sitting Bull's birthday party.

"It's quite romantic really, isn't it?" She sniffed.

"Oh aye, aye!" said Jock, for want of a better reply.

"Cliff!" shouted Ivan. "We'll put the ladder up against the wall. Come down carefully."

"Not unless she promises to marry me," yelled Cliff.

"I will darling. I will!" shouted Janet.

"All right then!" He put his foot on the top rung of the ladder, and began to descend slowly, with Ivan and Jock hanging on for grim death below. At last, he reached the ground, and Janet ran forward and flew into his arms. They kissed as the moon peeped from behind a cloud, casting its soft blue light on the scene of love reborn and hearts that once were sundered now replete.

"Quite, quite exquisite!" said Miss Farquaharson, as they left the lovers to rebuild their shattered romance.

"Will you be okay now, Janet?" Ivan asked.

"Yes, thank you so much," replied the girl, her eyes aglow with love for her beau.

Cliff turned to the pair, sobered now by the rush of adrenalin caused by his precarious descent.

"Thanks lads," he said proffering his hand.

Jock and Ivan said their farewells. And the happy pair slipped away into the shadows. A few seconds later, there came upon the breeze the sound of Cliff puking into a drain.

"Kind of spoils the moment, don't it?" Ivan observed. Jock muttered darkly as they shouldered the ladder.

CHAPTER EIGHT

Ivan's first period of nights eventually came to an end, and he was pleased to find that his next allocation was to be Male Eleven, where he would be under the auspices of Charge Nurse Ferdinand Harrison. He had met Ferdy previously and found him to be an amiable character.

Ferdy was an ex-coal miner, a past which he shared with many of his fellow Charge Nurses. Middle-aged and slightly balding, his well-preserved physique bore testimony to his pursuits of football and cricket in earlier years. He still enjoyed the odd game of cricket now, although he admitted to being a little slower between the stumps and less nifty in the field than in days of yore. He smoked an old meerschaum pipe and displayed to the world that outer serenity which seems to cocoon pipe smokers when they clamp the stem between their teeth and puff their aromatic fumes into a room. Only those who knew Ferdy well could see through this calm exterior to the maelstrom of life's troubles which lay beneath; for Ferdy had a cross to bear, in the shape of Sister Harrison, his overbearing and henpecking wife.

Ferdy, an inoffensive character, lived in dread of this ferocious female, nicknamed as the 'Dragon' firstly by her husband and subsequently by all who wondered how she could possibly be married to him. She ruled her ward with a steely glare and a vitriolic tongue.

Ivan had heard tales of her tyranny from the female students, and his heart went out to Ferdy whenever he heard her lambasting him on the telephone or saw her shaking her finger and stamping her foot at him in the grounds. This happened one morning as Ivan approached the ward door, where the Dragon was tearing a sizeable strip out of Ferdy's hide. Ivan slipped self-consciously past them and into the ward, narrowly avoiding being turned into two of sand and one of cement by the Dragon's Medusan stare. Ferdy broke off the engagement with the enemy and followed him into the office, where the student was somewhat bashfully reading the ward report book. The Charge Nurse allocated the other staff to their various tasks, asking Ivan to stay behind.

"Shut the door, lad," he said, in his soft northern accent. Ivan closed the door, and Ferdy motioned him to a chair. "Now then," he began, lighting his beloved pipe. "You may as well know that me an' t' owd lass don't hit it off too well. If I don't tell you, someone else is bound to, and I'd rather you heard it from me."

Ivan began to protest that Ferdy's marital problems were private.

"I know that, lad," Ferdy said, raising his hand to silence him, "but I tell all the new staff, and I expect you to bear it in mind if I'm a little 'tetchy' first thing in the morning."

"Look Ferdy, I don't really think" the embarrassed Ivan stuttered.

"That's all right, son! It's only fair that you should know about my system too, all the other lads do."

"What system's that, Ferdy?" asked Ivan, puzzled.

"It's what I call my early morning indicator," said Ferdy. "If you see me coming in at seven o'clock, try to see whether I'm wearing my teeth. If I am, everything is OK. If I'm not, I've had a bad night wi' yon cow, and it's best to keep out of my way until about half past ten!"

It was with due regard to Ferdy's warning that Ivan observed the status of the Charge Nurse's dental prostheses each morning. If all was well, Ferdy would shout a cheery 'Good morning!' as he entered the ward, flashing his toothy grin at all and sundry. If all was not well, however, he would collapse his features into that rubbery physiognomy that can only be executed by the totally edentulous. Such fine regard for the feelings of others rarely goes unheeded amongst Psychiatric Nurses, and Ferdy's staff displayed a loyalty to their Charge Nurse that was the envy of many of his contemporaries.

Ivan pushed the plate away, the meal was only half eaten. "What's the matter?" asked Dawn. "Don't you like my cooking?"

"It's fine love," Ivan replied, "but I'm rather full up."

"What have you been eating then?" Dawn asked, a little crossly.

Her parents had invited Ivan round for supper, and she had cooked the meal for him.

"Ferdy's 'special'!" Ivan grinned.

"What's that then?"

Ivan pushed his chair back from the table and moved to a comfortable chair by the fireside. Dawn's parents had gone out to the pub earlier, tactfully leaving their daughter to find the way to her man's heart in the time-honoured way, through his stomach! Dawn sat at his feet and he planted a kiss on her forehead. She looked up and smiled. Ivan began to relate the events of the afternoon to her.

"Percy!" Ferdy had called him from his office. He tended to call everyone Percy if he was unable to remember their proper name. The call was likely to be answered by any member of the staff, and Ivan had responded on this occasion.

"Yes, Ferdy?"

"Go down to the kitchen and tell Johnny, the head cook, that we have a Chinese patient who won't eat the food, and that I want a pound of rice."

"What's that for then?" Ivan grinned.

"Just do it, Percy, I'll show you what it's for later."

Ivan made off for the kitchen, mystified by Ferdy's request.

"Give Ferdy my regards," Johnny said, as he smilingly handed over the bag of rice. "And tell him that I'll have that recipe out of him one of these days."

Ivan relayed Johnny's message.

"He won't, you know," said Ferdy, with an air of mystery. He took the bag of rice into the ward kitchen, closing the door as he went in.

"Has Ferdy got the rice?" asked Eddie, the ward orderly.

"Yes, but what's it for?" Ivan replied.

"Every Sunday afternoon, he makes us one of the best rice puddings that you'll have ever tasted," Eddie said. "He won't let us know how he does it, but you'll see how good it is."

When the patients had finished their evening meal, and the dishes had been cleared away, Ferdie called Ivan and Eddie into the large pantry at the rear of the kitchen.

"Sit down lads," he ordered. Three places had been set at the small table, with bowls and spoons. Eddie winked at Ivan as Ferdy took the dish from the oven.

"I hope you like rice pudding, Percy?" Ferdy said to Ivan.

"I do indeed," the student replied, truthfully. Rice pud was one of his favourite dishes.

Ferdy spooned some of the pudding into the three bowls. The luscious, creamy aroma floated into Ivan's nostrils, stimulating his taste buds to mouth-watering anticipation.

"I'll warn you, if you're seeing Dawn tonight, Ferdy's pudding is an aphrodisiac," Eddie quipped.

Ivan grinned and took his first mouthful. Eddie had been right. It was good!

"How do you make it?" Ivan asked.

Ferdy lit his pipe, waved away curls of smoke and smiled. "You wouldn't make it right, even if I told you," he said.

Ferdie was approaching retirement, and the subject of how he would cope with the 'Dragon' without the escape route of going to work had been the subject of much speculation amongst the staff. The idea of them living together under each other's feet, was not one which anyone who knew them could take in.

One Sunday evening, after a particularly piquant rice pudding that had exceeded even its creator's expectations, Ferdy called Ivan and Eddie into the office.

"Now, I think I can trust you lads to keep a little secret," he said, drawing on the meerschaum.

The others looked at each other, both thinking that this was when they would learn the secret of the pudding.

"The fact is," Ferdy continued. "I've bought a little van. It's in one of the garages at the back of the boiler house. The Dragon doesn't know I've got it though, and I don't want her to." He stabbed at the two staff with his pipe to emphasise the need for secrecy.

"Well, we won't tell her!" Eddie said, a little affronted at Ferdy's apparent lack of faith.

"No, no, don't get me wrong, that's not why I'm telling you." He struck yet another match to rekindle the fire in the meerschaum. "You see, I've not driven since I was in the army. I've kept my licence up, but I'm a bit rusty. What I was wondering was, would you two be prepared to have a run out with me each evening, until I get a bit more confident?"

"Well, yes of course," Ivan asserted.

"You know we will," Eddie agreed, "but why all the mystery?"

"Ah well, that's just it you see. Let's just say I have my reasons and leave it at that for now. Now then, there's a set of keys for each of you. What I'd like you to do is to bring the van out of the garage and pick me up outside home. That way, the old cow'll think it's yours, and you can put it back in the garage afterwards. We'll just have a bit of a drive around the lanes and a pint or two afterwards. What do you say?" He looked pleadingly at his two colleagues, neither of whom could now refuse his request.

That was the way things went over the next couple of months. Ivan and Eddie settled into a well organised routine taking turns as Ferdy's unofficial driving instructors, until he could handle the little A35 with ease.

Ferdy's retirement party at The Nag's Head was one of those great social occasions which have gone down in history of many such occasions at the Meadows. Toasts were drunk, as were all the guests. The village streets rang with their merry songs as they staggered homeward after Ray, their genial host, had thrown them all out long after closing time.

The first day on the ward without Ferdy seemed a particularly sad one for Ivan and Eddie, both of whom were still suffering the after-effects of Ferdy's party. Ivan's thumping hangover added to his generally depressed mood as he and Eddie groaned at each other across the breakfast table.

"Hey! What do you think?" asked Vic, as he crashed his plate down onto the table with little thought for the suffering of mankind.

"What about?" Ivan asked painfully.

"Ferdy! The old sod's only loaded all his gear into a van and driven off into the dawn with the barmaid from the Nag's. The Dragon's having bloody apoplexy!"

There was something of a strange coincidence to follow these events, in that the replacement Charge Nurse for Male Eleven was known to be almost as bad 'henpecked' as Ferdy Harrison had been. Jack Bowie bore no resemblance to the hero of 'The Alamo' and inventor of the famous knife who was his namesake. A sharp featured little man with grey hair, Jack's distinguishing mannerism was his habit of pulling at his collar, as though it were about to tighten of its own accord and choke the life out of him. He was a born worrier, obsessed with the fear of making a mistake. He would check and double check everything that the staff did, always afraid that they would omit some essential task and expose him to criticism by the other shift. Whilst the staff found this failing of Jack's rather trying, he was generally well liked, being a kindly soul at heart. His wife was the night superintendent on the female side of the hospital and was sometimes referred to as 'The Other Dragon'.

Eddie avowed that he had once seen Jack measuring a Swiss roll with a ruler, to ensure that each patient received an equal portion. He was once reputed to have driven the ten miles from his home back to the hospital to lock a drawer. The night nurse who witnessed this event swore that the drawer was empty, and that Jack had told him that he could not have slept that night had he not returned.

To accept a lift in Jack's immaculately maintained Ford Popular was to volunteer for an ordeal. The 'Pop' was never renowned for its road-holding characteristics, and every gust of wind or stretch of uneven road would prompt Jack to screech the car to a halt. He would then get out, and walking slowly round the vehicle, would kick each tyre in turn shouting abuse and cocking two fingers up to the motorists behind. Having satisfied himself that none of the tyres were completely flat, he would pull into the next garage en route and painstakingly check the inflation pressures. His constant checking, whilst driving, that the choke was pushed fully in and the handbrake off would have made a saint swear, and the male nurses who were often his unwilling passengers were far from canonisation.

Ivan, Jock and Vic were strolling down the lane to the Nag's Head one night, when Jack's car hove to alongside them.

"Get in lads," he shouted. "I'll drop you off."

Having no polite excuse, the three reluctantly climbed into the car. After Jack ascertained that all the passengers were comfortable, and that they weren't bothered by the draught from the windows, and that the car's radio was not too loud, and that they were actually bound for the Nag's rather than elsewhere, Jack engaged the clutch, causing the car to leap forward and 'kangaroo' the first fifty yards down the lane. After squealing to a halt at the junction with the main road, he signalled left, then turned right. He gunned the little car up to its maximum speed of fifty-five miles per hour, and overtook a lorry, narrowly missing a bus coming in the other direction. By the time that they arrived at the pub car park, even the normally imperturbable Jock was showing signs of stress. Jack opened the doors, and the three lads stepped out onto terra firma, and in sheer relief that the journey had ended safely, Ivan invited Jack to join them for a drink.

"Thanks all the same, but I'd better not," he answered. "The wife's off duty tonight, and she'll be expecting me home."

The three made understanding noises, remarking without much conviction that they were sorry that Jack would be unable to join them.

"Oh well, perhaps just a quick one," he said, and led the way into the bar.

There was a party going on in the pub, as some of the students were celebrating passing their finals, and the ones who had failed were drowning their sorrows.

"Come and join us!" one of them shouted to the newly arrived foursome. "After all, it'll be your turn one day."

By the time that the fateful words 'time, gentlemen please!' had been called by Ray. The landlord, the whole bunch were well and truly 'in their cups' Jack included.

"What about the missus, Jack?" Ivan enquired.

"Sod the missus!" he replied, full of Dutch courage. "I'll bloody well tell her where she gets off if she starts on me tonight."

They all knew that Mrs Bowie outweighed and outreached Jack by some six stones and as many inches, and the sight of Jack telling her 'where she got off' was a difficult thing to imagine without smiling. Jack drew himself up to his full five feet four.

"The last time I had a night out with the lads was ten years ago. She clobbered me with the rolling pin that time. Well, just let her try it tonight. I'll bloody show her who's the boss!"

"Oh, you will, will you?" thundered a voice from the doorway.

Jack stood transfixed as he recognised the voice of his 'better half'. Slowly, and with an expression of dread, he turned, looking like a Christian who knew he was about to be thrown to the lions.

"Oh, hello Cuddles," he said, quaveringly.

"Cuddles!" burst out Vic, choking on the last dregs of his beer. Mrs Bowie fixed him with a glare that would have stopped a clock, then turned her attention to her hapless husband.

"So! This is where I find you, is it? I've just hired a taxi to look for you. I thought the car had broken down. You'd better come with me my lad; there are a few things that I want to say to you."

"Er, yes dear, right away dear," Jack stammered. He left with a worried glance at his colleagues as he followed 'Cuddles' out of the door. Full of sympathy for their comrade's plight, they all fell about laughing as Jack's 'Pop' kangarooed away into the night, the stentorian voice of Mrs Bowie booming over the roar of the tortured engine.

Little mention was made of the incident during the afternoon shift of the following day, which was just prior to Ivan's day off. He intended to spend the following day at home, and as he stood at the bus stop at the end of the shift, Jack's car drew up.

"Are you going to town?" the Charge Nurse enquired.

"Yes thanks," Ivan replied, hardly able to deny the fact.

"Hop in then!" Ivan settled into the passenger seat, and Jack took off in the usual manner. "I'm glad to have someone with me," he said. "It's my birthday. How about a quick 'un?"

"What about Mrs Bowie?" Ivan asked anxiously.

"Oh, that's all right tonight, she's on duty. She doesn't mind me going for a drink when she's on. It's just that she likes me at home early on her nights off. Come on, what do you say?" He looked pleadingly at Ivan, who had no heart to refuse.

They drove into town and stopped at the Market Inn. Jack insisted upon buying the first round, and, despite Ivan's protests, he bought the next one too.

"I know what it's like on a student's wages. You have this one on me!" They drank the second pint in virtual silence, Ivan being a little lost for words, as the memory of the previous night's proceedings dogged any attempt at conversation.

"Well, I'd better go and pay a call," Jack said at length.

He strode off in the direction of the 'gents' tugging at his collar. Ivan stayed at the bar and became engaged in a conversation with the landlord on the relative merits of the different brews on sale in the free house. Some fifteen or twenty minutes had elapsed before he realised that Jack had not yet returned. Anxious for his colleague's safety, he set off for the 'gents'. The way to the convenience lay through the lounge bar, where Jack sat engrossed in watching the news on the television set.

"Ah!" Jack said. "I'm sorry I've been a long time, kid, but I got interested in this."

"That's OK Jack," Ivan replied, resignedly.

He sat down to watch. At the end of the news, Jack bought another round. Returning from the bar with the drinks, he nodded in the direction of the TV

"They're OK, these, aren't they?" he asked.

"What are?" asked Ivan puzzled

"These televisions, of course," Jack said, thinking that the question had been neatly put.

"Haven't you got one at home, then?" Ivan asked.

Jack looked at him, a sadly philosophical look in his eyes.

"No, well, you see, the missus says that it's not worthwhile us having one, what with her working nights."

CHAPTER NINE

"Happy Christmas, darling," Dawn said, as Ivan kissed her under the mistletoe. They were in the staff dining room for their afternoon break.

"The same to you," he replied, thinking that he could grow to like this.

"I suppose this one's reserved, is she?" asked Tom Hanson, the rotund, jolly faced Charge Nurse who Ivan was currently working with in Ward five.

"Not for you," Dawn said, as she planted a kiss on Tom's bald pate, leaving a red imprint of her lipstick just to the rear of his frontal lobe.

"How about you two joining the rest of us at the Nag's Head later?" Tom asked. "Ray stays open until midnight on Christmas Eve."

"I can't, I'm afraid," Dawn replied. "I promised Mum that I'd help her with the turkey for tomorrow. I don't mind if you want to go, though," she said to Ivan.

"I shouldn't think you would," Ivan replied. "Who do you think you are, Mrs Bowie?"

Dawn playfully boxed his ear and left to go back to her own ward.

"She's a good 'un," Tom said, as she left him with a matching imprint on the left parietal lobe. "You want to look after that one."

"I intend to," said Ivan. "Who's going to be at the Nag's later on?"

"Everybody, just about. I'll be with Albert. I promised Ruth that I'd make sure he gets home safely."

"You're taking a lot on, aren't you?" Ivan asked, jokingly.

Albert, who Tom had referred to, was Albert Short, his lifelong friend and fellow Charge Nurse. Albert was well known for his affection for good ale, and this affection assumed romantic proportions during the festive season.

"Aye, mebbe," Tom said. "Are you going round the wards? We've not too much on at the moment."

It was the custom for the staff to tour the other wards at Christmas. Tom and Jock had been round the female wards earlier leaving a trail of giggling and squealing nurses behind them.

"OK I'll ring Vic, and we'll go together." Vic came up to 'Fives' in response to Ivan's call, and they commenced the tour with a visit to Bob Bracewell in Male Reception.

"I reckon we should win this year," Bob said, proudly. He was referring to the reception's entry in the annual competition for the best decorated ward. This was sponsored by the Hospital Management Committee, who awarded a small trophy to the ward which produced the most artistic and original display of Christmas decorations.

They were standing in the day room of the male admission ward. The patients were full of bon homie, sherry and mince pies, and most of them looked as though they didn't mind having to spend Christmas in hospital too much. Well looked-after under Bob's care at all times, they were especially well provided for during the festive season.

The walls of the room had been hung with large sheets of brown paper which were suspended from the high picture rail. The paper had been painted with a winter woodland scene, with trees and lakes and white capped hills in the distance. Father Christmas rode round and round the billiard table on his sled, a converted model railway engine, whilst Prancer, Dancer, Donner and Blitzen ran ahead led by Rudolph, whose red nose lit up every few feet. A miniature fountain played on one of the small tables, whilst a cardboard choir of angels on a window ledge sang carols through concealed speakers.

Ivan had to agree with Vic that this would take some beating, although he had heard that female twelve were in with a pretty good chance too. They set off in the direction of that ward to investigate, stopping off to listen as the Salvation Army band played for an excited crowd of patients and staff's children in the large car park. Snow began to fall, the flakes showing up in the glimmer of the lanterns held by the boys of the village church choir, as they carolled their way round the grounds. Dusk was gathering, and as the lights on the huge tree outside the main entrance were turned onto a chorus of 'oohs' and 'aaahs' from staff and patients alike.

At the end of the afternoon shift, Tom, Albert, Ivan and Vic bravely accepted a lift to the Nag's in Jack Bowie's car. Everyone was there, as Tom had predicted. Joe Joiner, Ron Mount, Bob Bracewell and all the other staff who were not on night duty were packed into the Snug, where Ray had laid on a free buffet for the hospital staff, a kind gesture which he had made for several consecutive years.

As the night progressed, all those present, began to get a little 'tiddly', none more so than Albert, who was 'tying one on' with a steel hawser.

"We'll have to watch him," Tom said with a look of concern. "I promised Ruth that I'd see him home, but I may need your help."

Ivan could see what he meant. Albert, a fairly large chap himself, was joining in Cossack dancing which was being demonstrated by Elmer, the huge Estonian Ward Orderly from male twelve. The floor shuddered as nearly thirty-five stones of male hospital staff whirled and kicked and leapt to the music of the accordion, played furiously by Jan, Elmer's equally gargantuan cousin.

By the time that Ray had once again shouted those dreaded words, "time, gentlemen, per-lease!" Albert was the tightest of a very tipsy bunch. He staggered out of the snug, colliding with the door post of the 'gents' as he entered that establishment.

"Oops, I mished!" he chortled. He found the gap on his second attempt, and lurched through.

"We'll have to walk home with him," Tom said. "He'll never get there alone."

As Albert emerged from the 'loo', Ivan took his right arm and Tom the left. "Come on, owd son," Tom said. "We'll get you home."

"Take me to my lovely Ruthie!" Albert said, a look of angelic bliss on his well-oiled countenance.

"His lovely Ruthie'll murder him!" Tom muttered.

Albert and Ruth lived in a Council house at the bottom of Chestnut Avenue, a tree-lined cul-de-sac. As Albert was 'legless', and neither of his escorts were too steady themselves, the trio did a complete lap of Chestnut Avenue, encircling every tree in the process. Their rendition of 'Hark the Herald Angels Sing' brought on bedroom lights and caused curtains to twitch in every home. At last, they reached Albert's front door.

"Where's your key?" Tom asked.

"I don't know. Where's my little Ruthie?" Albert carolled.

"Let's hope she's asleep," Tom replied, without much confidence.

Ivan propped Albert up against the pebble dashed wall and searched his pockets for the key. A comb, a pipe, pipe cleaners, tobacco pouch and coins came out before he eventually located it. He and Tom turned their attention to unlocking the door, hoping they could get Albert safely inside before Ruth heard the commotion and came downstairs to investigate.

Disaster struck just as they pushed the door open, Albert pushed himself away from the wall shouting, "Ruthie, darling." Pitching forward into the opposing wall. He slid to the ground, his face scraping on the wall as he did so, streaking the white pebble dash finish with his gore.

"Bloody 'ell! Tom exclaimed. As they carried him into the lounge and laid him on the sofa, Ivan turned on the light and surveyed the damage. A large abrasion on Albert's forehead was bleeding profusely, as was a small cut to his lower lip. His left eye was bruised and closing rapidly. Other minor cuts and bruises completed the carnage. Albert, however, was feeling no pain, and he treated them to a fine rendition of 'Nellie Dean'.

"Shut up, you soft bugger!" Tom ordered, as he bathed the wounds with cotton wool gleaned from a cupboard in the kitchen.

"I'm sorry, Tom, my oldest and dearest friend," Albert replied. "*Where we used to sit and dream, Nellie Deeean!*" he wailed.

A bump from upstairs jolted Tom into action. "She's coming down!" he hissed. "Let's get out of here!" They bolted for the front door abandoning their friend to his fate.

As they sprinted up the garden path, a light came on in the hall.

"You, drunken sod!" Ruth bawled. "You've been out with that bloody Tom Hanson again!"

"Give us a kish!" Albert replied.

"Gerroff, you bloody article!" Ruth yelled.

"The same every bloody Christmas," Tom said sadly. "He gets the enjoyment and I get the blame."

Albert came on duty on time the next morning, to Ivan's surprise. He wore a white swab taped over the abrasion on his forehead and sported a beautiful 'shiner'.

"Bloody Nora! What a night!" he groaned. "What happened?"

"You tripped over the pavement edge," Ivan lied. He could find neither the heart nor stomach to tell him the truth.

"Come up to my ward when you have your break," Albert said. "I've got something for you."

Ivan acceded to this request, arriving on the ward mid-morning. Albert presented him with a half-bottle of whisky.

"What's this for?" the lad asked in surprise.

"Let's say it's for services rendered," Albert grinned, now beginning to look more himself.

"I don't want all this!" Ivan protested.

"You needn't have helped me. There's a good many as wouldn't have," Albert winked. "I've got one for Tom as well."

Elmer and Jan, the large Estonian double act of that happy evening a couple of weeks before, were Ward Orderlies, employed to supervise the work of the gang of male patients who worked on the hospital farm. Between them, they and the patients worked the 150 acres of land, growing various crops and tending the prize-winning herd of Friesian cattle. Whilst the orderlies supervised the actual carrying out of the various tasks, the nurse accompanying the gang was there to keep an eye on the patients and monitor their behaviour. This task had today fallen to Ivan. He never minded doing this job during the summer, as he enjoyed the outdoor life, but his enthusiasm had waned a little on this particular morning, as he and a gang of patients chipped a three-inch layer of ice off the farmyard. This had to be done to prevent the treasured Friesians from slipping and injuring themselves as they were led in for milking. By the time the gang returned to the hospital, Ivan felt as though the blood had frozen in his veins.

"Are you cold, yunk mon?" asked Elmer in his fractured English, as they pulled off their working boots.

"Bloody frozen!" replied Ivan, with feeling.

"I gif you somethink!" Elmer said, opening his locker. He took out a bottle of colourless liquid, which he handed to Ivan.

"You drink!" he boomed. "Ees goot!"

Ivan sniffed the bottle suspiciously. "What is it?" he asked, not really wanting to know.

"Neffer mind vot it is, you drink!" Elmer commanded.

Ivan took a cautious swig. The hooch ran down his throat like napalm, scorching through his stomach, down through his abdomen and down the inside of his legs to his toes. He felt as though his whole circulatory system had boiled like the radiator of an old car. His throat was on fire.

"Strewth!" he gasped, when his scalp had dropped back on to the top of his head. "What's that?"

"Ah, goot, ja?" enquired Elmer. "Are you feelink warmer?"

"Phew!" Ivan said. "I'm on fire!"

"Estonia ees very cold place in vinter. Ve need somethink to keep us varm."

"Hell's bells." Ivan wheezed.

"Nein! Home brewed Vodka!" Elmer laughed.

"It's not bad." Ivan grinned, as the drink began to have its desired effect.

"More?" asked Elmer.

"Yes please." He reached for the bottle again.

"Nein, nein," Elmer boomed, snatching it away from him. "Leetle boys should not take beeg man's drink."

His massive frame shook with mirth at the student's instant state of intoxication. He corked the bottle and put it back into his locker.

By the end of the morning shift at two o'clock, Ivan was feeling decidedly tipsy, and all on two swigs of Elmer's patent remedy. Jock and Vic eyed their pal suspiciously as he sat pie-eyed at the lunch table.

"How'd you manage to get pissed on duty?" Vic asked, tactfully.

"Ask no questions, hear no lies," Ivan said, tapping the side of his nose.

"Where'd ye get the booze?" Jock asked, desperate for an answer.

"My lipsh are shealed!" Ivan slurred.

He rose and staggered forth from the dining room. Snow was falling as he made his way to his room in the male nurses' hostel. The snow whirled in his face, blinding him for an instant. He reeled and fell forward, hitting his head on the ground. Stars burst before his eyes, and he lapsed into unconsciousness.

"Are you OK kid?" asked a familiar voice, as the light returned.

"Where am I?" he asked, groggily.

"In Male Reception's clinic," Albert replied. Ivan now also recognised the grinning features of Bob Bracewell. He sat up on the examination couch whereupon Albert and Bob had deposited him.

"Albert found you and brought you in," Bob informed him. "We've patched up your face."

Ivan put a hand to his forehead and felt a strip of sticking plaster there.

"Thanks Albert," he said, as he remembered what had happened.

"That's all right," Albert said. "You owe me half a bottle of whisky!"

CHAPTER TEN

Ivan was now entering the final nine months of his three years of training. He and Dawn were planning to get engaged when he had passed the state final examination, which was looming in front of him in the October of that year. He still had his motorbike, but he hadn't used it very much over the winter, as Dawn didn't like riding pillion in the ice and snow.

In time, the winter snows gave way to spring sunshine, and Ivan sadly pushed the bike out of the shed. His sadness was brought about by the fact that he had somewhat reluctantly decided to sell the machine in favour of a cheap car.

"The time has come to put aside childish things," Vic quoted, as Ivan lovingly polished the glowing red paint and bright chrome bike for the last time.

"If you don't want your skull rent asunder with this spanner, you won't extract the urine!" Ivan grinned, swinging the implement at his friend's head.

Vic ducked the blow.

"Anyway, I'm sure you'll find the back seat of a car more conducive to the alleviation of your baser instincts," he said.

"Cheeky sod!" Ivan riposted. "Still, you've got a point," he said, thoughtfully.

"What are friends for, if not to sweeten the bitter pill of disappointment with the sugar of enlightenment?" Ivan ignored the remark, knowing that Vic would hold forth interminably if he showed any sign of appreciation of his friend's poetic nature.

The bike was duly sold, to another student who promised to give it a good home, and Ivan began to scan the small ads in the local rag for a suitable vehicle. They all appeared to be a little too costly, as he had to allow for sufficient funds for tax and insurance out of the proceeds of the sale of the bike.

He spent his day off at home that week, and was sitting in his father's favourite armchair reading the paper when Ike came home from work,

"What's this then; got the sack?" asked the aged parent.

"I'm looking for a car," his son informed him.

"What sort of a car?"

"Preferably one with four wheels and an engine," Ivan quipped.

Ike thought for a few seconds, "There's a chap at work trying to sell one, you might have a look at that."

"What is it?"

"A Ford Popular,"

Ivan looked doubtful. He had suffered too much at the hands of Jack Bowie to allow any great enthusiasm for the 'Pop'.

"I don't know," he said.

"Please yourself, but it's a good 'un," his father replied. "I could ring him if you wanted to see it."

"OK, then. We'll go after tea."

"Pulls like a train," said Reg, the owner of the Pop, as he put it through its paces. "You'll have a bargain at forty-five pounds."

"Thirty!" shouted Ivan, over the roar of the ancient side valve engine.

"Forty!" yelled Reg.

"Thirty-five!" Ivan bellowed,

"Done!" Reg took his hand off the wheel to shake on the deal, and the Pop, lurched sickeningly.

"That's the one bad point with these," Reg explained. "They do tend to roll a bit,"

"I know!" Ivan replied, as he recalled Jack's car wobbling round corners.

"Well, there we are then," Reg said as he pulled up outside Ivan's parents' home.

Ivan counted out thirty-five pounds in five-pound notes, and Reg handed over the logbook.

"I hope you'll be happy with her," he said. "She's been a good 'un to me." Ivan dropped him off outside his house a few minutes later, and Reg took one last sad look at the car.

As Ivan bade Reg goodbye and drove away, he began to feel pleased at buying the car, particularly when he visualised idyllic drives into the country with Dawn. He arrived back at home, to find his father waiting on the doorstep.

"Well, what do think of her" Ike asked, casting a critical eye over the rusting bodywork.

"She'll do for a couple of years," Ivan said, optimistically.

Ike said, "Come on, you can take me for a pint." He climbed into the passenger seat.

Ivan pulled the starter button, and the engine chugged into life. He set course for the Nag's Head, intent on showing off his purchase to the lads.

(This all was, of course, several years before the introduction of the 'breathalyser'!).

"What's that knocking?" Ike asked, as they drove up the steep hill which approached the village from the direction of the town.

"What knocking," Ivan asked in return, pretending not to hear.

"Sounds like a little end," Ike offered.

"It's probably the tappets," Ivan said, trying to suppress the uneasy feeling that the sound produced in his mind.

The weeks passed by, and the knock didn't seem to be getting any worse. Ivan eventually learned to ignore it, rather as one ignores the ticking of a clock.

His buying the Pop seemed to start a fashion. Within weeks, many of his fellow students, staff nurses and others began to come to work in 'bangers' of all shapes and sizes. Ford Pops, Austin Rubies, Morris and Standard 8's seemed to abound. The nurses had recently received a two and a half percent pay rise, but Ivan had found himself to be ten shillings a week worse off, as the board and lodging charge had been increased by thirty percent as part of the same round of pay bargaining. Any new affluence as a result of the pay award was decidedly conspicuous by its absence, and it was this subject that occupied the thoughts of Ivan, Jock and Vic as they drank their beer that night.

"It's all very well having a car, but can you afford to run it?" Jock asked.

Ivan smiled at his Caledonian friend's concern for his finances. "It all depends on how far I go in it," he said. "Obviously I won't be going to Blackpool every day, and if I can't afford the petrol, the car will have to stay in the garage."

"I wouldn't want to go to Blackpool on any day," Vic announced. "I think it's a bloody awful place."

"There's a bloke who can afford to run a car," Ivan observed. He was referring to Reg Black, the proprietor of the local garage, who was sharing a joke with Ray at the bar. Reg was well known to the staff of The Meadows, as he had often been called to the hospital to start a recalcitrant engine on a cold winter's night. He always attended to such a task with good humour and courtesy, and he usually charged reasonable fees to nurses.

"Why don't you tap him up for some more discount?" Jock asked, his mind, as always attuned to thrift.

"Why should he give me any discount?" Ivan grinned.

"Let's ask him," said Jock. "Here Reg, will ye no join us for one?"

The garage owner looked round for the source of the shouted invitation.

"Hello Haggis," he said, cheerily. "To what do I owe this honour?"

"We were just wondering if you would be prepared to offer us a little discount, in recognition of our roles as pillars of the community?" Jock told him, with tongue in cheek.

"Cheeky Blighter!" Reg said. "What's in it for me?"

"The guaranteed custom and allegiance of me and my colleagues," Jock replied. "We would promise to trade exclusively with you for all our automotive requirements: unless we could do better elsewhere, that is."

Reg laughed. "I don't know! I've had some propositions in my time, but this one just about takes the biscuit. I'll tell you what. Buy me a drink and" I'll think about it."

"Done!" said Vic, wresting Reg's glass from his grip.

"Aye, ye may be!" Jock muttered.

They exchanged small talk and banter for a few minutes whilst Vic bought the round, then Reg said, "I'll tell you what I'll do. You three start a staff motor club, and if you get more than twenty members, I'll issue them all with privilege cards entitling them to five percent off petrol, spares and servicing. How's that?"

"Make it ten percent," Ivan said.

"Five per cent, take it or leave it," Reg said, firmly.

"OK," said Ivan. "We'll see what we can come up with. Now, as a gesture of good faith, I propose that Reg buys the next round!"

"Seconded!" Vic laughed.

"Bloody 'ell!" said Reg, good naturedly. "Any more deals like this one, and I won't have a business to give anyone discount from. What're you all drinking?" He took the glasses and took them to the bar.

Ivan looked at Jock and grinned.

"Business is business!" Jock said, with hands outstretched and shoulders hunched.

"He's the first Jewish Presbyterian I've ever met!" Vic said.

A few hastily drawn posters placed around the hospital brought in well over the required number of prospective members. A trip by Ivan to the printing shop in the Occupational Therapy Department secured a cheap source of membership cards. A committee was formed and held its inaugural meeting rather noisily in the Snug at the Nag's. Ivan was elected chairman, Vic secretary, and Jock became the natural choice for treasurer.

"What is the club going to do, besides twisting Reg Black's arm?" asked Tom Hanson.

"We're looking for suggestions," Ivan sagely replied, not really having an answer.

"What about a Treasure Hunt?" someone at the back shouted.

The idea met with an enthusiastic response, and Ron Mount, who had once been an amateur rally driver, was co-opted to organise the event.

"The idea is," Ron explained. "That the contestants follow a course laid out for them on a handout in the form of a series of cryptic clues. As they go round the course, which will be about twenty-five miles from start to finish, they will be required to collect various objects or items of information as evidence that they have visited certain points on the route. For instance, a beer mat carrying the name of a particular pub, or the name of the vicar of the church, as displayed on the notice board. Marks will be awarded on the basis of the number of clues solved correctly, and the number of items of 'treasure' collected. In the event of a tie, the team coming home in the quickest time will win. You will leave the hospital gates at timed five-minute intervals."

"The club will provide, from the funds, a sandwich supper in this room at the end of the event. That will obviate the need for any of you beer swilling sods to risk losing your licence en route. Jack Bowie and I will plan out the course, and we start at two o'clock on Sunday afternoon."

Ron sat down to a chorus of cheers and ribald remarks. The Meadows Motor Club was born!

They assembled at two o'clock on a beautiful Sunday afternoon, in the large hospital car park. Dawn was on duty, leaving Ivan in need of a navigator. Whilst on the one hand, he hoped that some gorgeous female nurse would be assigned to his car, he also feared Dawn's possible reaction to such an occurrence. The names of all the drivers without a partner were put into a hat, and those unattached navigators were put into another one. The teams were selected by Matron, who had graciously consented to draw the names in pairs, one from each hat.

Having made a short, complimentary and thoroughly uninteresting speech, Matron drew the name of the first driver.

"Alf Smith," she shouted. "Will be navigated by June Brownlow."

A chorus of jeers, catcalls and wolf whistles arose from Alf's good fortune in 'drawing' the delectable June.

"Jock McCracken," Matron announced. "And Sally Wilson." More jeers, etcetera as Jock somewhat bashfully escorted the equally delightful Sally to his mobile rust heap.

"Ivan Reader," Matron trilled. "And Vic Murdoch."

Cries of "Shame," "Hard Luck," and, "Oooh, Ducky!" arose from the multitudes, as Ivan signalled his disapproval of the draw by holding his nose and performing the action of pulling a lavatory chain.

Vic muttered an obscenity into his ear, gave the crowd a 'V' sign, and took up his seat to a storm of apathy from the assembled populace.

"Just my bloody luck!" Ivan exclaimed, but without much malice.

"It could have been worse," Vic replied.

"How's that?"

"You might have drawn Matron!"

Ivan saw the logic of this argument, and he laughed as he started the engine and moved the car onto the 'grid'. As their turn came round, Ron Mount checked his watch then waved them away. Ivan gunned the Pop down the lane at a breakneck thirty-five miles per hour, and Vic opened the sealed envelope of clues.

"What's the first one?" Ivan asked.

'You'll climb the hill where the road does twine,

And drive to the village named for swine', Vic read.

"That must be Hoggington," Ivan said. "It's up a hill about two miles south of here, and the road twists and turns as you enter the village."

"Let's check the next one," Vic suggested. "It might strengthen the lead."

Ivan drove towards Hoggington as Vic unfolded the road map, then read the next clue.

'A spire and gate along by here. Remind us all of Christmas cheer'.

"That's it!" Ivan said. "The church at Hoggington is St Nicholas', the German Santa Claus."

"So far, so good," Vic observed.

A few minutes later, they arrived outside St Nicholas', just as Jock and Sally were leaving.

"Either he's wrong too, or we're at the right place," Ivan said.

"The next clue is a question," Vic said. "Who died on October the 18th 1897?"

"That must be on one of the gravestones," Ivan said.

They entered the church yard and began to read the inscriptions on each stone in turn, looking for the key date. As they did so, Bob Bracewell and Alf Farmer arrived at the entrance.

"We'd better get a move on!" Ivan prompted.

They wound their way through the stones, but nowhere could they find one carrying the pertinent date. Suddenly, Bob and Alf sprinted for their car, jumped in and drove away.

"They must have found it, down by the gate," Ivan said.

Arriving under the lich gate, the pair looked round for the elusive date. Suddenly, Vic pointed upward.

"There it is!" he yelled.

Ivan craned his neck. Vic was pointing to an inscription on a board above the gate.

'In loving memory of the Rev. Samuel Cuthbertson, Vicar of this Parish for thirty years. Passed from this life October the 18th 1897'.

"Write it down," Ivan said, running for the car. "What's the next one?"

'Go west, young man and climb again.

You'll get a tan whilst up this lane'.

Ivan looked blank. "Strewth!" he said. "I don't know what that is."

He stopped the car whilst they consulted the map. They followed the line marking the road which ran west from Hoggington.

"That's it!" Vic said, stabbing at the map with his finger. "Sunny Hill!"

"I hope you are right," Ivan said. "It's a long steep road, and I don't fancy driving the old heap up there on a wild goose chase."

"Come on, we're wasting time," urged Vic

Ivan drove off, and as he did so, he found that he was suddenly more conscious of the knocking sound which he had grown so used to hearing.

"That's funny," he said, a little anxiously.

"What's funny?" asked Vic.

"That noise."

"I can't hear anything," Vic replied.

"Sssshhhhh! Listen!" Ivan hissed. The knocking was definitely growing louder. "I don't like the sound of that!" he said, now getting really worried.

"It doesn't sound any worse to me," Vic said, "but I don't know very much about cars."

"Neither do I," Ivan said, "but I know it's getting louder."

"Nah, you're just imagining it," Vic said, trying to reassure his friend, without much hope of success.

Presently, they reached the foot of the very steep haul up Sunny Hill, and Ivan accelerated as gently as possible, trying to coax the old car to the top. He knew that he could coast down the other side, and if the worst happened, there, there would be a telephone box in the village from which he could summon help. As they approached the brow of the hill, he was suddenly seized by a strange feeling of impending doom. He fought with his innermost fears, telling himself that he was probably exaggerating the problem, when disaster struck. A loud 'bang' and a rattling sound came from under the bonnet, and the Pop ground to a halt.

"Blimey! What was that?" Vic asked, anxiously.

"I don't know, but it sounded bad," Ivan replied. He got out of the car and lifted the bonnet. As he did so, a cloud of oily smoke poured out. As it slowly cleared, he spotted a growing pool of oil on the road beside the car.

"Bloody 'ell!" he exclaimed. "It's a big end, I think!"

He crouched down and peered under the car. As he had feared, a shattered piston and connecting rod dangled obscenely from the hole that they had blown through the sump as they burst out of their cylinder. Oil and water poured from the hole. "Oh shit!" Ivan said, out of sheer exasperation.

"Is it serious?" asked Vic, innocently.

"I'll say it is!" Ivan venomously replied. "It means either a new engine, or the car is finishing up on the scrap heap."

Well, I did say that I didn't know much about cars," said Vic.

They walked to a telephone box, from where he rang his father. Ike reached them an hour or so later in his own car, and he towed the crippled Pop back to the Meadows, where they pushed it sadly into its garage. Ivan was feeling fairly 'down in the mouth', as he doubted whether he could afford to have the car repaired.

"In any case," he said to his father. "The body's not so good. I don't know whether it's worth fitting a new motor in it."

They stood and surveyed the car in silence.

"What's up wi' it?" a voice said from behind them. Ivan turned. An elderly man stood there with his hands in his pockets, a cigarette butt dangling from his bottom lip.

"Hello Fred," Ivan greeted him. Fred was a patient in Male eight and had been in hospital for over ten years.

"A big end's come through the bottom," Ivan informed him, not really expecting him to understand.

"Aye, I see it has," Fred said, peering underneath the car. "Tha's bin lucky, mind; thy crank's none broken."

Ivan looked at the old chap with interest.

"Do you know something about engines then, Fred?"

"I ought to," the patient said, with a faint smile. "I was a mechanic for forty years. I'd just retired when t 'missus upped and died on me. That's what bought me 'ere; that an' t' bloody ale." He coughed violently and crushed out the cigarette with his boot. "I'll tell thee what," he said, in his north country accent. "If tha gets a set o' pistons an' shells, I'll shove 'em in fo' thee!"

Ivan looked surprised. "Are you sure you can manage it, Fred?"

Fred looked insulted in return. "Tha what? I was repairin' these buggers when tha were in thy cradle! Tha get t' parts, an' I'll show thee. I'll need tools, mind."

"I could borrow a socket set from the fitters," Ivan said.

"Aye, all reet! Tha get 'em, and we'll soon 'ave yer gooin' again. I'll see thee!" He walked away, coughing on yet another 'fag'.

"What do you think," Ike asked, when the old man had gone.

"I don't know," Ivan said, rubbing his chin thoughtfully. "I'll ask his Charge Nurse."

"Oh yes, he'll do it for you," Albert Short told Ivan. "You won't have to rush him though; he likes to take his time over the job. He put a new set of piston rings in my old bus last year. She's never used a drop of oil since."

And take his time he did! Every day for the next fortnight, Fred tinkered away at the old engine, fitting the new parts with care and precision. He would disappear under the car for a few minutes at a time, emerging frequently to light another Woodbine, cough, and catch his breath. Eventually, the task was completed. Fred turned the engine over slowly with the starting handle.

"That feels reet enough," he said. "Start 'er up, but don't shove thy clog down too 'ard."

Ivan pulled the starter button with some trepidation, and the engine immediately purred into life, sounding smoother than Ivan had ever heard it before.

"Aye, she'll be gradely now," Fred said. "Just tha treat 'er gently for the first couple of 'undred miles."

Ivan turned off the ignition and got out of the car. He fumbled in his rear trouser pocket and pulled out a five-pound note.

"Here, this is for your trouble," he said, offering the note to Fred.

Fred looked at the note, then at Ivan. "Tha can put thy bloody money away," he said. "I don't want owt."

"But—" Ivan began.

"But bloody nothin'," Fred said, angrily. "If I can't do thee a bit of a job, like yon, it's a poor how d' ye do. Anyway, I've enjoyed it, tha knows! It makes me feel as though I'm p'raps not on t' bloody scrap 'eap after all. Tha just gi' us a packet o' fags, and we'll call it straight."

CHAPTER ELEVEN

The spring progressed into a long, hot summer. Ivan found it strangely paradoxical to be looking across the sun-baked fields that only months before, had been two or three feet deep in snow. Then, the icy winds had blown across the south midlands plain, piling the powdery snow into dune-like drifts. Now, on this shimmering July afternoon, Ivan and Dawn sank down weary from the heat onto the bank which bordered the southern edge of the hospital cricket fields.

As he lay on his back looking at the blue sky, with Dawn playfully teasing him by tickling his ear with a feathery stalk of grass, Ivan kept thinking of the old song *The Playing Fields of England*. The click of bat on ball and the scampering footsteps of an outfielder on the bank above his head added to the illusion that he was on the green lawns of an old English public school, rather than in the grounds of a psychiatric hospital.

"Gaudeamus Igitur, tum-te-tum-te-tum-te-tee," he hummed.

"What's that?" Dawn asked, breaking his reverie.

"What's what?" He had been suddenly and somewhat self-consciously jerked back to reality by her question.

"That song you were humming," Dawn said.

"Oh that! Just something I heard once. It's an old school song actually."

"What your school?"

"No," he laughed. "Hardly Derfield Sec. Mod! More Eton or Harrow I think."

"You've been watching too many old films on the telly," Dawn laughed, immediately latching on to the line of thought that had led Ivan into humming the tune. That sort of thing seemed to be happening between them quite frequently these days.

"Oh, I don't know though," Ivan said, sounding slightly hurt. "I was just thinking that this must qualify as a grade 'A' typically English summer's day.

"Yes, I thought that's probably what was in your mind," she said. "The staff here are hardly typically English though, are they?"

"No, I suppose you're right," he said. Suddenly, he grabbed her round the waist, pulling her down beside him in a flurry of flouncy lace petticoats, squealing and giggling in mixed delight and embarrassment.

"Behave yourself!" she rebuked him, sitting up and brushing dust from her attractive cotton dress. "You'll spoil my clothes."

"Take them off then," he grinned.

"That's enough!" she laughed, springing to her feet and running away from him. He chased her along the bottom of the bank, until she finally let him catch her at the rear of the cricket pavilion. She squealed delightfully as he grabbed her.

"Put her down you lecherous sod!" came a voice from the pavilion. "You're disturbing the players." Vic emerged from round the corner, his wide grin causing Dawn to blush.

"I might have known that you'd be somewhere around," Ivan said, in a falsely complaining tone. "Anyway, why are you wearing whites?" he asked, remarking on his friend's attire.

"Because, old boy, I have been given the honour of being asked to go in to bat for our ailing hospital side against the 'Drum and Trumpet', the team who are currently at the top of the league."

"Is that a-i-l-i-n-g or a-l-e-i-n-g?" Ivan asked.

"Probably both," Vic grinned.

"I didn't know you played cricket," Dawn said.

"I haven't played since I left school," Vic told her. "They were a man short for today, and Arnie asked me to turn out when I met him in the Nag's last night." He was referring to Arnie Majors, a Charge Nurse who had acted as secretary, manager and coach to the hospital cricket team for over fifteen years.

A splatter of applause from the field signalled the end of the fifth batsman's innings.

"That's me in next," said Vic, taking his leave of them.

"Let's go and watch," Ivan said. "I could do with a bit of a laugh".

He took Dawn's hand, and they climbed up the bank and went round to the front of the pavilion.

"Hello, you two," Arnie said, simultaneously giving Dawn an approving looks up and down and giving Ivan a wickedly knowing wink

"How are we doing?" Ivan asked him.

"Not so well," Arnie said. "We're seventy-six for five, in reply to their 247."

"Demon bowler, eh?" Ivan asked.

"'Fraid so. They've got a chap who would make Truman look slow. It looks as though Vic's got a strike against him now."

Vic emerged from the pavilion and walked across the pitch to a chorus of good, humoured barracking from Ivan, Arnie, Jock and Bob Bracewell, who had brought a party of patients from Male Reception to watch the game. Vic raised his bat in mock salute, suppressing the inevitable 'V' sign in deference to Dawn's presence. Arriving at the crease, he took 'middle and leg' from the umpire and made his mark. Looking up, he visibly quavered as he caught his first closeup of the opposing bowler. He was a giant of a man, at least six foot three tall, with broad shoulders and a tanned, leathery complexion. He grinned wickedly at Vic as he tossed the ball from hand to hand.

"Ready son?"' they heard him say, in a booming voice. Vic nodded nervously and took up his stance.

The bowler seemed to take hours to walk to the far end of his run up, where he turned, then began to thunder down the pitch like a runaway locomotive.

"*Strewth*!" Ivan murmured, as he contemplated his pal's impending doom. The bowler let fly, and the ball bounced viciously, short and fast. Vic lashed out blindly at it, and by some miracle, the bat connected. Driving the ball over the bowler's head with incredible force. The bowler ducked, and the ball landed about twelve feet over the boundary, sending a small group of patients scuttling for their lives. The home supporters erupted into applause as Vic's six went up on the scoreboard.

A fielder retrieved the ball, and the bowler again began the long trek to the start of his run up, after first giving Vic a withering glare. He thundered up to the popping crease once more and unleashed a cannon ball delivery. Stumps and bails flew in all directions and Vic began to walk back to the pavilion.

"Good grief!" Arnie moaned. "That's the end of anything like a batting order on our side".

His words proved to be prophetic, as the fast bowler made short work of dismissing the remaining wickets. The players took tea in front of the pavilion, Dawn helping the other ladies to serve them. Ivan sat on the grass by Arnie, as the Charge Nurse gloomily munched his sandwiches.

"We could do with one more batsman and, a fast bowler," Arnie said. Tom Hanson who had also brought a group of patients down, joined them.

"What about Harry?" he asked. Arnie brightened.

"Yes, of course! I'd forgotten about Harry."

"Harry who?" Ivan asked.

"Harry Robson, the patient from Male Ten." Ivan could vaguely remember Joe Joiner telling him that Harry had once played for the County, and that he had occasionally turned out with the staff team. "I'll nip up there and see if I can persuade him to play," Arnie said.

He returned as play was about to commence, accompanied by Harry, who had been hurriedly 'kitted out' in Arnie's old whites. Arnie quickly cleared the substitution with the umpires and the opposing Captain, and the players walked out for the second half of the match.

Harry was put on to bowl against the openers. Ivan and Vic watched with interest as Harry walked down his run up. He turned and ran briskly down to the crease. As he brought over his right arm, he suddenly let out a blood curdling howl. The batsman flinched, completely unnerved. The ball shot under the bat and took the middle stump cleanly out. The batsman stood transfixed, speechless with surprise and confusion. He looked to the umpire for a decision, but even that worthy gentleman was quite obviously at a complete loss.

"I say!" the batsman called out as he ran to the umpires. "That's not allowed, is it?"

The umpire said nothing, but he walked over to consult his colleagues at square leg. They spoke for several minutes, with several gesticulations. Eventually, they called both Captains over to where they stood.

"We're not sure about this situation," the square leg official said, "but we recall nothing in the rules which refers to a bowler making utterances as he delivers the ball. We have decided, therefore, to give the man out." He turned to the captain of the Drum and Trumpet tea. "If you are not satisfied with this decision, you may, of course, appeal to the County Board."

"I most certainly will appeal!" the captain said, with marked umbrage. "Never in my entire twenty years in the game have I witnessed such a thing."

"But the man was clean bowled," Ron Mount, said in defence of Harry. "Surely you can make some allowance. After all, our chap is a patient here you know."

The opposing captain looked unhappy. "I don't know," he said. "I appreciate that the chap may be unwell, but really—"

"Gentlemen, gentlemen!" the umpire said. "The decision now will have to stand. As this is a friendly match, and no loss of points is involved, I suggest we continue with the game. The board will give a ruling for future reference, should you so desire."

The other captain looked aggrieved. "I mean," he said. "Hang it all! We're playing this lot in the challenge cup next week, and if these are the tactics they employ, well really—" He disconsolately returned to the pavilion, and the game restarted. Ron had a quiet word in Harry's ear, and the patient bowled from then on in perfect silence. The damage had been done, however, and it took only slightly more than an hour for Harry and the other bowlers to dismiss the rest of the team. Fortunately for them, bad light stopped play, and the match was abandoned without a result.

The following afternoon, Ivan was in the kitchen of the male staff hostel when the doorbell rang. He went to the door an opened it, curious as to who it could be that had not followed the usually accepted practice of simply walking in. A dusky faced stranger stood at the threshold with two large suitcases.

"Excuse pliz", he said. "I am told to report to thees abode, where I will be conducted to my room."

"Really?" asked Ivan, amused at the newcomers over precise use of the English language. "And who might you be?"

"Ah, excuse pliz. I am Aziz Jahore," the stranger said, nervously.

"Well come in Aziz," Ivan said, "and we'll sort out which room you're in.

Aziz stepped inside. "I beg your pardon," he said. "But I am obviously not expected. I had previously assumed that my arrival would have been notified to you by Mr Hunting. I see now that I have been foolishly precocious, and for this I sincerely apologise." He bowed, formally.

"That's all right." Ivan laughed. "Would you like some tea? You look as though you've had a long journey."

"Thank you. That would be most acceptable." Aziz bowed again, and Ivan had great difficulty in restraining himself from returning the gesture.

Ivan made the tea and carried the tray into the common room, gesturing to Aziz to follow him. They sat down. "Have you any more luggage?" he asked.

"There are some things at the station. Later, I must return there and collect them."

"Do you mean Derfield station?" Ivan asked.

"That is correct."

"Well, it's a ruddy long way to walk," Ivan said. "I'll tell you what; have your tea, then we'll go down in my car and pick your stuff up."

Aziz grinned widely, his white teeth appearing to glow against the background of his dusky countenance.

"That is most kind of you." He rose and bowed to Ivan yet again.

Ivan laughed. "You'll have to get out of that habit. You'll give us all lumbago!"

Aziz looked most unhappy. "I am sorry if I have offended you."

"Forget it!", Ivan smiled. "Just try to be a little less formal. There are blokes living in here who still drink their tea out of the saucer!"

Aziz looked puzzled but said nothing. Whilst Ivan found Aziz's impeccable manners strangely disturbing, he felt rather sorry for the young man, who was obviously a little overawed by the new situation he found himself in.

"How long have you been in England?" he asked, trying to penetrate Aziz's almost painful reserve.

"I arrived last week," Aziz said. "I have been staying in London with my brother and his wife. Mr Hunting was most kind to offer me an appointment on the strength of a reference from my last employer in Colombo. I am given to understand that he and my father are acquainted."

"I see!" said Ivan. "Look, you stay here and drink your tea and I'll give Mr Hunting a ring. We'll see if he can tell us which room to put you in. There are a few empty at present." He went to the internal telephone in the hall and dialled Mr Hunting's number.

"Hunting!" said a curt voice at the other end.

"Hello Mr Hunting," Ivan said. "There's a Mr Jahore here at the hostel. He says that you've taken him onto the staff. I wondered which room you may have reserved for him?"

"Ah yes!" said Mr Hunting. "That'll be young Aziz. I hadn't expected him until tomorrow. Look, would you do me a favour? Sort out an empty room for him and I'll see him in my office at nine a.m. tomorrow. If you're free, perhaps you could escort him over. He's the youngest son of my old batman from when I was in Ceylon during the war. Old Jahore was an excellent chap. He wrote to me a few weeks ago to see if I could offer Aziz a post. I was glad to help. If the boy is anything like his father, he should settle in well."

Ivan said, "He seems a little unsure of himself at the moment."

"Yes, I expect he'll feel a bit strange at first. Apart from that, the Singalese, or Sri Lankans as they are now known, are almost painfully polite, but thoroughly good chaps for all that. Once you get to know him, and he you, I'm sure he'll settle in."

Ivan laughed. "Yes, I had noticed that! He keeps bowing!"

Hunting laughed. "Yes, that sounds about right! OK then, if you'd do the honours and bring him up to see me in the morning, I'd be grateful".

"Leave it with me," Ivan said, then hung up.

He found an empty room and helped Aziz to deposit his belongings. Half an hour later, they were in the left luggage office at Derfield station. Aziz had a large trunk, which they managed to squeeze into the rear seats of Ivans Pop, and also a cricket bag.

"Hello!" Ivan said. "I see you're a cricketer!"

"I do like to play," Aziz answered. "But I don't anticipate playing during this season. Firstly, I must find a team who are willing to offer me a place."

"No problem!" Ivan said. "The hospital team are crying out for players. Are you any good?" He smiled as he asked the question.

Aziz looked a little uncomfortable. "I had the honour of playing for my college at home, although I was usually in the second team only."

"Ah well, I expect you'll shape up. Come on, we'd better get back and have some tea."

They drove back to The Meadows and went directly to the dining room. Jock and Vic were sitting together at one of the tables, and Ivan introduced his new companion to them. They did their best to make him feel welcome, but they found this heavy going in the face of Aziz's almost disconcertingly impeccable manners.

Ivan and Jock went to the servery to fetch some tea, leaving Vic trying vainly to engage Aziz in conversation.

"Perhaps he'd relax a little over a pint?" Jock suggested.

"I don't know whether he drinks," Ivan said, doubtfully. "Still, I think it's worth a try. How about inviting him to join us in The Nag's later on?"

"Good idea!" Jock said. "If Ray's bitter won't help, there's no hope for the lad!"

They all arrived at The Nag's Head later on that evening, to find Arnie Majors looking glumly into his glass.

"Hello Arnie," Vic said, cheerfully. "What's up?"

"I was just sitting here brooding on life's cruel habit of slapping a bloke down, just when he's thinking that things are on the up!" he said.

"Hello, hello! This sounds like a man with a problem, gentlemen!"

"I've got eleven bloody problems," Arnie said. "That bloody team we played last week — we walked all over them last season, and I was quite pleased when we were drawn against them in the challenge cup. I hadn't realised they'd signed a bloody tame gorilla as a fast bowler. That big bloke 'll tear us to pieces next Sunday. I just wish we had a decent batsman to go in with Big Ron as joint opener, to use up the big feller's overs. If we could do that, we might just get into the final yet."

"Yes, of course. It's the semi-finals next week, isn't it?" Vic said.

"Don't remind me!" said Arnie. He looked at Aziz in faint surprise. "Who's your friend?"

Ivan introduced Aziz to Arnie, and they shook hands. Again, Aziz's retiring manner tended to slightly dampen the moment.

"Where are you from?" Arnie asked, trying to draw Aziz out of his shell.

"I am from Colombo," Aziz told him.

"Colombo, eh?" Arnie said, with genuine interest. "I was there in 1946!"

"Were you in the same outfit as Mr Hunting?" Ivan asked.

"Yes, I was. We had known each other at The Meadows before we enlisted of course, and it was a strange coincidence that whilst we never met during hostilities, we ran into each other in a bar one night. Bob was a second lieutenant, and I was a sergeant. We spent quite a bit of time together back then, but we haven't really maintained the friendship in England. Different circumstances, you know?"

"Did you ever know Mr Hunting's batman?" Ivan asked.

"Did I?" Arnie said, loudly. "I wish old Jahore was here now. He was the finest batsman I've ever seen in action. He'd have clouted that big daft sod all over the bloody field!"

"Small world, isn't it?" Vic said, winking at Ivan and the others.

"What do you mean?" Arnie asked, suspecting that he was being taken for a ride.

"Anyway, what made you ask about the Governor's batman?"

Aziz opened his mouth to speak, but was silenced by Jock pressing his finger to his lips.

"Oh, no particular reason," Ivan said, nonchalantly. "I think he once mentioned that the bloke was a good player."

"Go on!" Arnie scoffed. "When did you ever get pally enough with Mr Hunting for him to tell you that?"

"Oh, it must have been that night when he invited Jock and me round for dinner," Ivan said, with an air of aloofness.

"Bullshit." Arnie laughed. "You'll be telling me next that you're his secret love child!"

Ivan managed to look distinctly rattled by Arnie's rhetorical rejoinder, drawing gales of laughter from Vic and Jock. Poor Aziz looked puzzled by the line that the conversation had taken.

"How about giving Aziz here a game, Arnie?" asked Vic, changing the subject.

"I don't know," Arnie said, eyeing Aziz doubtfully. "Is he any good?"

"Plays for India," Ivan said, recovering his usual good humour.

"Oh yeah?" Arnie sneered. "India rubber?"

Aziz looked disconcerted but said nothing. "Seriously though, he could come down for net practice?"

"I suppose so," Arnie said. "It's too late to pull anything out of the bag for next Sunday though! We'll just have to say goodbye to the cup for this year!"

"Do you know?" Ivan began. "It's Arnie's supreme confidence and fortitude that should serve as an example to us all. With men such as this to lead us, why should England tremble?"

"Balls!" Arnie laughed. What are you all drinking?"

Aziz politely requested a pint of India Pale Ale, and in doing so, quite unknowingly got marked as 'one of the lads'!

Aziz appeared at the practice nets the following Wednesday evening, resplendent in his whites. His pullover bore the emblem of his college team in Colombo, and the fine bat that he carried bore evidence of much use.

"Go into the second net," Arnie directed him, "and I'll send you a few balls down."

Aziz took his stance in the net, and Arnie bowled an awkward leg break at him. Aziz played the ball with ease. Arnie then bowled a succession of spin and pace deliveries, and Aziz played them all with the same consummate ability.

"When are you going to test him out?" Vic called to Arnie's annoyance.

No bowler likes to have every ball played so disdainfully. Picking up the ball, Arnie walked a long way out of the entrance to the net.

"Try this one for size, Son!" he called to Aziz.

He sped down his run and unleashed a fearsome delivery that dropped viciously short. Aziz executed a perfect cut, and the impact of the ball into the side netting almost demolished the structure. Arnie was now flushed with ire. He delivered several faster balls, alternating with spin, and Aziz dealt comfortably with them all.

"Jock!" Arnie shouted. "Nip up to Male Ten and bring Harry down!"

Harry appeared at the nets a few minutes later, accompanied by Joe Joiner and Jock. Harry, who often played for the staff team although himself being a patient, fired delivery after delivery at Aziz, who parried every ball with ease.

"Ah reckon you're onto summat there!" Joe said to Arnie. "You'll 'ave to give the lad a game next Sunday. He'll gie that big bugger what for!"

"How about letting Aziz go in with Ron to open the batting?" Ivan asked Arnie.

"No bloody fear!" Arnie reposted, with mock disgust. "I'm going in with Aziz myself. Ron will be third man!"

The Meadows won the toss on the Sunday, and Arnie elected to bat first. He took first strike himself. He nervously parried the first five balls from the gargantuan fast bowler, who had the scent of an opening maiden over. Arnie must have sensed this, and he tried to drive the sixth ball through the covers. The ball snicked the outside edge and trickled down towards third man. Arnie began a run that could only be described as suicidal, but Aziz set off like a hare from the other end, touching his bat to the crease just as the stumps were felled by a wickedly accurate return. Arnie, eighteen years older than Aziz and three stones heavier, was caught with two yards to go, torn out by his own recklessness. The giant had his wicket maiden!

Arnie returned to the pavilion wearing a sullen expression, scarcely glancing at Ron Mount as he went out to join Aziz.

He glared at Ivan as he reached the pavilion. "So much for your bloody mate!" he said, with uncharacteristic venom.

"What do you mean?" Ivan asked, surprised at Arnie's attitude.

"If he'd run when I shouted, I'd have made it!"

"Now hold on Arnie!" Ivan protested. "He was in a good way before you were. You ran yourself out!"

Arnie slunk off into the locker room to take his pads off. Meanwhile, Aziz was preparing to face his first ball from the demon bowler. The big man retraced his by now well-worn steps, turned and ran swifter than ever, it seemed to Ivan. His right arm came over like a ballista, and the ball rocketed down the pitch with perfect line. Aziz stood his ground and patted the ball away for no run. The bowler assumed an air of satisfaction and prepared for his next delivery. This time, he ran a little slower and Aziz raised his head very slightly. As the bowler let fly, the breath exploded from him in sheer exertion. The ball dropped short, bouncing viciously. Aziz hooked, and the ball flew straight and level across the playing area, not losing any height until it crossed the boundary. The umpire signalled 'six' to the scorer, and the Meadows supporters clapped cheered and hooted.

"What's going on?" asked Arnie, drawn from his dark retreat by the noise.

"Aziz has just belted the big lad to kingdom come!" Ivan told him.

"No — go on?" Arnie said, incredulously.

"I should watch this — you might learn summat!" Joe Joiner observed, as he joined them.

The celebration in The Nag's that night was loud and long, with Arnie making a speech, praising Aziz's skills with both bat and ball and apologising for his own pique earlier in the day.

Mr Hunting joined the party as Aziz was being carried round the room shoulder high, much to his Sri Lankan embarrassment.

"I think he'll settle in now!" Ivan shouted to Mr Hunting over the strains of *For He's A Jolly Good Fellow*.

The Chief smiled in reply. "Yes, I think you're right. It was bound to happen once he got on a cricket field. It's all in the genes you see!"

CHAPTER TWELVE

The three-monthly staff changeover came around once again, and Ivan was not displeased to find that he had been placed on Male one, with Arnie Majors as his Charge Nurse. The ward had recently been modernised ('upgraded') and it now accommodated twenty elderly gentlemen. Forming a part of the frontage of the hospital and overlooking the extensive rose beds and the sports field through a picture window which ran down a complete side of the ward, the patients and staff had a panoramic view of the grounds, the sports field and the surrounding countryside. Outside a large pair of glass doors, a low walled terrace provided an idyllic outdoor sitting space for the ward's elderly residents, and they would while away the summer afternoons under the colourful café type parasols which surrounded the circular metal tables.

Ivan and Arnie's first shift together was on the first Sunday afternoon of the new rota. This proved to be another of the bright, warm days which had so far characterised that summer. They met at the handover meeting, when the morning shift passed on all the relevant information to the oncoming late shift.

Tom Hanson, the Charge Nurse of the opposite shift, had also moved to Male one that morning, and he was speaking to Arnie as Ivan entered the office. The routine business of the ward having been dealt with, the two Charge Nurses turned the conversation to the subject of cricket.

"Are you playing this afternoon?" Tom asked Arnie.

"Yes. Are you?" was Arnie's rhetorical reply.

"What's this then, the Geriatric Ashes?" Ivan facetiously interjected.

Arnie laughed, cursing the student for his irreverence. "It's the 'Old Boys' match. We play the police retired officers' team every year. This will be the fifth year since we started. It's 'even Stephen's' so far, with two wins to each side, so we'd like to win this one."

"But you're on duty," Ivan observed.

"Ah yes, but Mr Hunting will be playing too, you see? He's asked me to bat 'last man', so I'll only be down there for the last wicket. They'll have to manage with one less fielder."

He continued, "You'll be able to watch my innings from the terrace. When you see my wicket go down, run the bath, so that I can get straight into it. I'll leave my uniform in the bathroom. I'd be grateful if you'd put a clean towel in there for me too."

"I'll be hanging on your every move!" Ivan mocked.

"Hmm! Well don't forget that the patients will require your attention too!" Arnie said. He left for the bathroom, where he would change into his 'whites'.

Ivan busied himself around the ward, and emerged onto the terrace with some of his elderly charges at three-forty-five p.m. just in time to watch Arnie walk out to the crease with his bat under his arm, with all the dignity of Bradman going into bat at Lord's. He walked back across the field approximately three minutes later, having fallen victim to Sergeant Morris' slow left arm spin at the first ball. He walked back to the sun terrace as planned, entering the ward via the French windows, and retiring straight into the bathroom, which Ivan had prepared (or so he thought) as instructed.

Whilst Arnie soaked his aching limbs after his arduous two minutes at the crease, Ivan continued with his game of dominos against a surprisingly sharp-witted octogenarian. Five minutes later, Mrs Gladys Harbottle JP, the chair of the Hospital Management Committee, came into the ward from the corridor entrance, accompanied by two gargoyle like ladies wearing flowery hats.

Ivan rose from his seat and introduced himself to Mrs Harbottle, who he had only previously seen from a distance. He decided that this was by far the best way to view the grand lady, as in closeup, she looked even more grotesque than her two companions.

"Good afternoon, young man," she said, in a voice that sounded as though she was sucking a large pebble. "These two ladies are friends of mine from the Women's Institute. I would very much like to show them around this lovely ward, if that would be convenient?"

Her expression left Ivan in no doubt as to what his answer should be, so he offered to escort them. Mrs Harbottle dismissed him with largesse, much to his relief.

She turned to the woman on her left, who looked as though she had recently completed a tour of duty on the roof of Notre Dame.

"Of course, I chose the wallpaper, carpets and curtains," she said.

"Very nice, I'm sure," the other lady said, in a tone which suggested she was anything but sure.

Mrs Harbottle either missed or ignored the implication and swept on into the dormitory. She was just describing the agonies of the artistic task in choosing the wall coverings, when the sliding door of the bathroom crashed open and to Ivan's horror, Arnie emerged, stark naked, with his back to the ladies.

"Where's me bloody towel?" he yelled.

The chips were now well and truly down, and Ivan had to think quickly.

"Come on back into the bathroom old Son," he said loudly, putting his arm round Arnie's shoulder in an attempt to inject some modesty into the situation by shielding the bewildered Charge Nurse from Mrs Harbottle's baleful eye.

Arnie, who now fortunately grasped the full horror of the predicament, played along.

"Yes, I'm sorry nurse!" he said tottering back into the bathroom in a masterly imitation of a confused old man.

Ivan slammed the door shut, almost ruining Arnie's wedding tackle in the process.

"And who, pray, was that?" Mrs Harbottle demanded.

"I'm sorry ma'am," Ivan said. "But the Charge Nurse is off the ward at the moment, and the old gentleman insisted on taking his bath now. I tried to persuade him to wait until later, but he can be quite difficult."

"Yes, yes, I can quite see—" Mrs Harbottle blathered, obviously wondering what tittle tattle would buzz through the WI as a result of this incident. Rallying admirably, she turned authoritatively to her two companions.

"Come, ladies!" she commanded. "We'll take tea in the boardroom. I'm sure you must be in need of some refreshment."

They left, and Ivan dashed back into the bathroom, collecting Arnie's towel on the way.

"You bone headed bloody idiot!" he seethed. "Why didn't you warn me that the old bag was in the ward?" He snatched the towel angrily and began to rub furiously at his damp skin.

Ivan was alarmed at first, but the rear view of Arnie bending over and drying his legs convulsed him with laughter. Arnie rounded on him angrily, and then, seeing the funny side of the situation began to guffaw himself.

Albert Short, who had come into the ward to borrow some equipment, stared in disbelief at the scene before his eyes. There was Arnie, naked as the day he was born, collapsed in hysterics on the white painted chair in the bathroom, with Ivan equally overcome with mirth at the door.

Albert helped himself to the equipment and muttered, "It's a bloody queer place, this is!" as he stomped off in disgust!

Arnie started two weeks' holiday at the end of the month.

"Are you going away?" Ivan asked him over a pint in The Nag's that evening.

Arnie answered, "No, can't afford it, I'm afraid. I'll have plenty to do though. The missus wants a wall built at the bottom of the garden."

"Gonna brick the fairies in, are you?" Ivan quipped.

"I'll bloody brick you in if you're not careful" he said, in mock anger. "No! You know there's a brook at the bottom of the garden?"

"Oh yeah?" Ivan replied.

"Yes, well, the gardens all slope down towards the brook, you see, and every time we have heavy rain, the topsoil and the small plants get washed into the brook. All the neighbours have built retaining walls, and Ethel has been on at me for years to do the same. I had hoped that the soil would level itself out eventually, but it seems to be getting worse. So, I've ordered the bricks, sand and cement etcetera and it should arrive early next week."

"I'll wish you the best of luck then!" Ivan said, lifting his pint in salute.

"Thanks, but I'll need more than luck. How are you fixed for giving me a hand?"

"Who? Me?" Ivan said, choking on his beer. "I've never laid a brick in my life!"

"Neither have I!" said Arnie. "But I expect we'll learn! Tell you what. Why don't you tap up a couple of hefty patients from Male Ten to cart the bricks around the back. I'll give them a couple of quid for their help!"

Ivan thought over the proposal, then said "OK! I'll get Joe Joiner to sort out a couple of likely lads, then you can give me a ring on the ward when the stuff arrives. I'm on mornings this week, so I could help you in the afternoons."

With the plan sealed, the conversation returned to the usual topic of cricket for the rest of the evening.

Arnie's call came on the Wednesday morning. "There's a bloody big heap of bricks and sand here," he said. "I think we may need three of Joe's lads to help us move it. See if you can borrow a big barrow from the gardeners."

"OK!" Ivan replied. "I've got Harry and Sam lined up, and Joe said he'd lend a hand himself if we needed him. We'll see you later!"

Ivan rang off and dialled Male Ten to speak to Joe to confirm the arrangements.

The four of them arrived at Arnie's abode at about three o'clock in the afternoon. Ethel greeted them at the front gate.

"He's not very happy," she said, raising her eyebrows meaningfully.

"What's up wi' 'im?" asked Joe, in his usual gruff tone.

"George has a bad back, so he can't come. I told him to leave it, but you know what he's like. He won't be beaten!"

She turned and went into the house, whilst Ivan, Joe, Sam and Harry made their way to the back garden. Arnie was digging the foundation trench for the wall, red faced and sweating profusely in the hot sun.

"Thank God you've come!" he said, climbing out of the trench, the course of which he had marked out with stakes and string. "Here Harry, you're a good bloke with a spade. Carry on digging this trench out Son, whilst we go and fetch the bricks etcetera round here."

Harry went into the trench and began to dig with all the same level of gusto that he showed when bowling.

Arnie straightened up painfully and looked at Joe. "I suppose you've come to gloat?" he grinned.

"Who me?" Joe snorted. "Now I ask yer. What do yer mek o' that? Yer come to gie a bloke an 'and, an' he insults yer afore yer get started!"

"Never mind Joe!" Ivan grinned. "He'll thank you when it's done!"

"Aah should bloody well think so, an' all!" Joe grunted, loading bricks into the barrow.

Ivan grinned at Arnie, who playfully stuck out his tongue behind Joe's back.

By six p.m. the wall had grown to a height of two feet above the ground. Ivan considered that they had done well, but Arnie's temper had not been improved by all the jibes that Joe had poked at him during the afternoon. Ethel came down with the third tea tray of the project.

"Well, are you satisfied now then?" he asked her, a little niggardly.

"Hmm!" Ethel said, doubtfully. "I suppose it's all right."

"What do you mean by 'all right'?" Arnie asked, with considerable ire.

"Well, it's not quite straight, is it? she asked, comparing the line of the wall with the one in the neighbour's garden.

"She's raight, yer know," said Joe

"It looks all right to me!" Arnie barked. "Anyway, who's bloody side *you* on?" He glared at Joe, who winked at Ivan who was having great difficulty in preventing himself from laughing. He knew from his own experience that Joe was never happier than when he was playfully 'needling' one of his colleagues.

"It ain't bloody straight!" Joe said, pointing to the wall.

"Oh, bugger it! It'll do!" Arnie said, clearly piqued. Harry and Sam withdrew tactfully to a safe distance, obviously expecting sparks to fly.

"Well, if a job's worth doing, it's worth doing well!" Ethel said. "Mr Brown next door has made a lovely job of his. And he didn't have as much help as you."

"Oh! I see!" roared Arnie. "Well why didn't you go and ask him to bloody well build it for you then?"

"Don't you shout at me, you great lout!" Ethel yelled. "What will the neighbours think?"

"Sod the bloody neighbours," thundered Arnie. To Ivan's alarm, he ran forward and took a flying kick at the wall, which, due to the still wet mortar, slowly collapsed into the brook. Arnie let out a yell of pain and fell to the ground clutching his foot.

"Arnie!" Ethel shouted in alarm. She ran to his side and took his head into her hands. "I'm sorry love. I didn't mean to complain."

"Bloody 'ell" Arnie grimaced, as Ivan pulled off his wellington boot and sock. Arnie's big toe was swollen and inflamed. Even the normally imperturbable Joe winced when he saw it.

"Will it be all right if we go now, Mr Joiner?" asked Sam.

"Aye OK lads," said Joe. "Ah'll see yer both in the mornin' an' square up wi' yer."

The two patients left the painful scene, and Joe turned to Ivan.

"We'd best put a cold compress on it first, to bring down the swellin'. Go in the 'ouse and see what yer can find!"

Ivan ran to the house, returning a few minutes later with a bowl of water into which he had put some ice cubes, along with some gauze swabs and a narrow bandage which he had managed to find.

Joe soaked the gauze in the cold water and wrapped it around Arnie's toe, displaying surprising dexterity and gentleness. He secured in in place with a short piece of the bandage.

"'Ow does that feel nah then?" he asked Arnie.

"Not too bad now, thanks Joe," Arnie replied, looking a little more comfortable.

Joe gently moved the toe from side to side, causing Arnie to wince a little. "Yow've bin bloody lucky yow've not broken it," he said. "It'll gie yer some 'gyp' fer a couple a days though. Nah, sit in the barrow an' we'll take yer in the 'ouse."

Arnie painfully mounted the barrow and Ivan wheeled him down the path. With one arm around Ivan's shoulder, Arnie hopped from the kitchen door to the sofa in the lounge, where he gratefully sank down. Ethel pressed a large glass of whisky into his hand, wiping away her tears.

"I'm sorry love" she sniffed.

"That's all right, it was my fault," Arnie replied.

"Well, I'll leave you two love birds and see what Joe's up to" Ivan said.

He walked down the garden, to find Joe carefully replacing the last few bricks, which he had retrieved from the brook, onto the wall.

"That's good!" Ivan said. "You did a good job on the toe as well."

Joe looked up with one of his rare half smiles. "Ahrr! Well, I keep tellin' yow young un's that yer don't know it all. He looked towards the house then looked back at Ivan".

"Bugger a bloke as can't 'old 'is temper thought!"

They repaired to The Nag's Head for a well-earned pint.

CHAPTER THIRTEEN

Ivan stood at the bus stop by the hospital gates one Friday afternoon. His objective was to get the Market Inn in the cattle market, as it stayed open until five p.m. on market days to slake the thirst of the local farming community. He knew that some of his pals would already be in the bar when he arrived.

The bus was a few minutes late, which was fortunate for Joe, a patient from Male Twelve, as he called to Ivan whilst sprinting across the tarmac towards him.

"Are you going into town?" Joe asked.

"Yes, do you want be to bring something back for you?"

Joe grinned one of his toothy grins. "Yes please. I'd like half an ounce of that light shag rollin' tobacco — you know — the one I usually have." He handed Ivan some money.

"I'll be back on the four-forty-five," Ivan told him.

Joe grinned again, whistled, then squeaked through his clenched lips, squeezing Ivan's cheek between his thumb and forefinger.

"Gerroff, you daft sod!" Ivan laughed, pushing Joe's hand away. He was one of Ivan's favourite characters amongst so many in the hospital whose eccentricities had an amusing appeal to many of the staff. Many of the patients knew that there was much to be gained by developing these characteristics, and it was a skilful Nurse or Psychiatrist who could discern between this deliberately acquired behaviour and the type which was produced by a combination of psychosis and long years of institutionalisation. Bob Bracewell had once described Joe as 'every man in the street's impression of a lunatic', and whilst Ivan felt that this was putting the case a little too strongly, there was no doubt that Joe did his best to live up to his image.

Joe's flaming red hair stood on end, seemingly illuminated by his ruddy complexion. His bright-blue eyes stood out like the proverbial chapel hat pegs, whilst his toothy grin bore a remarkable resemblance to a piano keyboard. When the whole effect was taken into consideration, 'eccentric' was the mildest adjective that could be used to describe Joe, harmless as he was!

After a slight overindulgence in the excellent bitter ale served up by Roger, 'mein host' of The Market Inn, Ivan set off around the various tobacconists in search of Joe's particular band of 'old and nasty'. He had often noted, on such occasions, that fresh air enhanced the effect of Roger's liquid masterpiece, and there seemed, to Ivan, to be rather a lot of fresh air in Derfield that afternoon. There was so much of the stuff permeating his respiratory system, in fact, that he found some difficulty standing up straight as he waited on the platform in the bus station for the arrival of the 15A. Far from causing him any concern, the situation seemed to amuse him, and it was his unsteady gait and silly grin which added to the discomfiture of the rather anxious looking lady who was also waiting for the bus.

The lady rebuffed Ivan's friendly smile with a pronounced sniff and turned her back on him. Ivan, ever watchful for someone who may be in need of his services, had noticed her trepidation, and felt compelled to help her to cope with the pressures of life. *After all!* He thought, *he was almost a fully qualified Psychiatric Nurse, and he ought to be able to use his skills to try to allay this lady's innermost fears.*

"Hello!" he said, giving the lady another one of his cheery smiles when she eventually looked his way again. The lady's look of apprehension deepened so Ivan tried again. "Nishe day, isn't it?" he said, attempting the English method of starting a conversation. The fresh air now seemed to be affecting his pronunciation. He thought this was strange, as he was perfectly clear in his own mind as to what he had tried to say.

The lady was feeling even more nervous now, as it seemed that this rather inebriated young man was waiting for the same bus as herself. Steeling herself to this possibility, she resolved to sit as far away from him on the bus as possible, and to call the conductor if he proved to be at all troublesome.

The bus duly arrived, and the lady boarded, making her way to the rear seat. She realised almost at once that she may have committed a serious tactical error, as the young man had lurched down the aisle and sat down heavily beside her, cutting off her escape route.

"I say!" Ivan said. "Do you mind if I join you? There aren't usually many people on the bus at this time of day, and you looked as though you needed cheering up a little."

"I suppose it's all right!" She sniffed, turning her head away. She stared resolutely out of the window as the bus pulled away, not turning until the conductor came along.

"Fares please," he said, his bright green turban contrasting sharply with the red décor of the bus.

"Does this bus go all the way to The Meadows Hospital?" the lady asked him.

"Oh yes indeed ma'am," the conductor replied. We are going directly to the main gate. It is jolly good service I am thinking, yes indeed." He punched a ticket and handed it to her in exchange for the fare. "Holding very tightly please. I am telling you when we are getting there."

"That's OK", Ivan said. "I'm going there myself. I'll tip the lady the wink when we dock."

"Jolly good!" the conductor beamed. "I am thinking that all this tipping, winking and docking are making life easier for my humble self. I will be much obliging for this sharing of my burden!"

"No trouble at all old boy!" Ivan replied. "You just bring us in safely from the bridge and I'll act as first mate."

The conductor took up his station by the cheery looking West Indian driver, and Ivan turned his attention to the lady's worries.

"So, you're going to The Meadows too, are you?" he asked.

"Yesss," she answered, uncertainly.

"Ah good! You'll find it a very friendly place. You'll be given the very best of care and attention."

"Whatever do you mean?" she asked, sharply.

Now it was Ivan's turn to realise his own tactical error. He had thought, from her nervous demeanour, that she was presenting herself as a patient.

"I say, I'm most frightfully sorry," he said. "I thought you were going there for medical reasons. Please forgive me if I have embarrassed you."

"I should think so too," she said. "Coming from you, if you don't mind me saying, that's a good 'un!"

"Er, excuse me!" Ivan said. "What do you mean by 'coming from me'?"

"Well, aren't you one of the inmates?" she asked.

Ivan thought for a moment the grinned. "Oh, I see! You thought that I was a patient and I thought you were about to become one. I should think that makes us about all square, doesn't it?"

For the first time, the lady smiled. "I suppose it does. No, actually, I have an appointment with the Matron about a cleaning job."

"Really?" Ivan said. "Well, I'm sure that you'll enjoy working there. I certainly do."

"Oh, you work there too, do you? What are you? A clerk or something?"

Ivan laughed. "Not exactly. I'm a Student Nurse."

"Oh, I see," the lady said. "Of course — I hadn't thought. I bet you need to be able to look after yourself, don't you?"

"Not particularly. We get fairly well looked after you know?"

"No, I didn't mean like that. I meant with these inmates in there!"

Ivan smiled reassuringly. "Actually, we don't refer to our clients as 'inmates'. They are patients, and we have very little to worry about from them."

"Hmmm!" the lady said. "Well, I don't know, I'm sure. I wasn't too happy about coming up here in the first place, but you know what they're like at the labour exchange. If you don't try for a job every so often, they stop your dole money."

Ivan grinned. "There's absolutely nothing for you to worry about, dear lady. I doubt very much, if you passed one of our patients in the street, that you'd give him a second glance."

"It's all right for you to say that!" She frowned. "But I've never had anything to do with this sort of place before. I mean, you hear such funny things, don't you?"

"Do you?" Ivan asked. "What sort of funny things?"

"Well — you know!"

"No, I don't!" Ivan said.

"Oh of course you do! My sister visited someone here years ago. She said it was awful. The nurses had to unlock the doors to let her in. And how the poor soul was being treated —

having to sit there amongst all those mad people! She turned funny after having a baby. Thought it was Napoleon's child or something. It was one if my sister's neighbours. Well, I mean, they're more to be pitied than blamed I suppose, but honestly, I don't think I'd feel too safe myself!"

"Madam!" Ivan said sternly — or as sternly as Roger's bitter would allow. "I can only reassure you once more that there is nothing at all to fear. In my experience, the patients of this hospital are completely harmless, and are, in fact, completely normal people for the most part. True, some may be more seriously afflicted than others, but even then, any violent tendencies are merely of a transient nature, and we are very well trained to deal with them."

The woman started, visibly, and Ivan realised that he had just undone all of his previous good work. From her expression, she was even more terrified than before.

"Oh my God! Violent tendencies! I knew I should never have come here!"

"Madam, madam!" Ivan said, trying to calm her down. "Will you do me the honour of allowing me to escort you to Matron's office? You will then see that there is nothing at all to justify your concern."

"Well, that's very nice of you, I'm sure. After all, if you're a male nurse, you ought to know what you're talking about I suppose!"

The bus trundled down the hospital lane, and Ivan kept his companion engaged in conversation until it pulled up at the terminus.

"Oh dear!" the lady said. "I don't think I'll bother after all. I'll just get back on the bus and go straight back to town."

"Now look!" Ivan said, with such authority that he surprised both himself and the lady. "If you see anything at all to frighten you in the next ten minutes, I'm a Chinaman!"

"Very well then," she said, uncertainly. "You lead the way then!"

They passed through the main gates into the grounds, and Ivan could see that she was as impressed by the view as he had been himself some two years earlier.

"What a lovely place!" the lady said. "I'd really no idea!"

Ivan smiled the smile of the self-assured. *After all!* he thought. *What could possibly frighten anyone here?* The birds sang in the trees, and all around them was an air of peace and tranquillity.

As they walked towards Matron's office, Ivan asked her again, "Now, what is there to be afraid of here?"

He didn't need to wait long for an answer. As they rounded the corner to the admin block, Joe ran up behind them.

He threw his arms around Ivan, squeaked through his lips and said loudly, "Have you brought my tobacco sirree?"

Ivan smiled. "Yes Joe. Here it is." He put his hand into his pocket and handed the package to Joe.

Joe whooped. "Wheee! You're a bloody good 'un. I'll have you made president for this!"

The woman stared transfixed for a few seconds. Before Ivan could stop her, she turned on her heel, sprinted for the bus and was on it and gone down the lane before he could martial his thoughts.

"What's up wi' 'er?" Joe asked.

"I don't know, I'm sure!" Ivan said. "Tell me Joe, could you see me with slanted eyes, dressed up in a white overall and a tall hat, with a wok in my hand?"

"A what in your hand?"

"A wok!"

"Wot's a wok?"

"Never mind mate!" Ivan said. "There's some funny folk about, you know?"

Joe was to feature in an event a few weeks later that was destined to become one of those gems of folklore which are passed down by word of mouth through generations of nurses. Ivan had found one of the few things which could get under the skin of the normally imperturbable sub species 'Chargenursus Belicosus' was (and still is!), the 'do-gooder'!

There are many very genuine and sincere people who freely and generously devote much of their lives to helping the mentally ill in various voluntary capacities. The range of activities which such people involve themselves is extremely wide, from simply visiting the many patients who are not visited by their families, to taking them into their own homes, organising holidays and generally providing the 'icing' on the 'cake' which is provided by those who work in the system — doctors, nurses, social workers and many others.

The 'do-gooder', however, is a bird of a very different plumage. These are that small minority who seek to gain personal esteem by involving themselves in these activities and then telling all and sundry what wonderful people they see themselves as being. This approach arouses antagonism in the professionals and often among the patients and generally does far more harm than good.

Mrs Barton-Fanshawe was just such a blot on the escutcheon of The Meadows' small army of reliable and trustworthy volunteers. She described herself as a 'devoted worker for the amelioration of the suffering of those less fortunate'. Joe Joiner described her as a pain in the arse — an opinion which was shared by many others.

"She'll be here tonight, I suppose," said Jim Tweedie, the Charge Nurse of Ivan's shift on Male Twelve.

"Who's 'she'?" Ivan asked.

"That bloody woman," Jim replied.

"Oh, you mean 'B.F'!"

"Who else would I describe in such glowing terms?" asked Jim, with a wry grin.

"Who indeed?" asked Ivan, in return, with a sardonic smile.

Mrs Barton-Fanshawe had taken upon herself the task of visiting patients in female and male wards twelve, the wards which housed the few most disturbed patients in the hospital. A large, overdressed and overbearing woman, she constantly criticised both staff and patients, claiming always that she had a finer appreciation of the needs of the patients than the nurses, or, indeed, the patients themselves. The sight of her approaching with her encrusted costume jewellery, her 'beehive' blue rinsed hairstyle, flowered hat and horn-rimmed spectacles was usually the signal for the staff to suddenly busy themselves with some urgent task. They would do this to escape from her withering glare and falsely assumed tones of refinement (or 'refainment', as she would have pronounced it).

At seven o'clock, she entered the ward, sending staff and quite a few patients scarpering in all directions. Ivan and Jim, involved in a four-way game of snooker with two patients were unable to escape, and it was this unfortunate pair that she now bore down on.

"Good evening, Mrs Barton-Fanshawe," Jim said politely.

"Ay would laike to see the following patients," she said, rudely failing to return Jim's greeting. She reeled off a list of names, starting with Billy Walters. Billy was one of those patients, who, whilst he presented the staff with some problems in managing his often violent and unpredictable behaviour, also elicited a good deal of sympathy from them. He had been admitted at the age of thirteen, having been completely disowned by his parents. He was of sub-normal intelligence, and would have been more appropriately placed in a hospital for the mentally handicapped. He had originally been admitted as an emergency following a severe beating from his drunken, oafish father. Like so many 'short-term' admissions, he had become a lifelong resident of The Meadows.

"I don't think that Billy is well enough to be visited at the moment," Jim informed 'B.F'.

"And may I ask why not?" she enquired, officiously.

"I'm sorry, but I can't discuss that with you Mrs Barton-Fanshawe", Jim replied. I have to respect the patient's confidentiality."

"But surely—" she began to protest.

"I'm very sorry," said Jim. "But that's the way it will have to be!"

He broke off the engagement by retreating to the office. Mrs Barton-Fanshawe, plainly annoyed by what she considered to be Jim's dismissive attitude, pilloried one of the other unsuspecting souls on her list and proceeded to tick him off for not wearing a tie. Ivan, fighting a powerful urge to knock off her flowered hat and jump on it, joined Jim in the office.

Jim was sitting at the desk, glaring through the window. Ivan knew that Jim was generally a genial soul, not given to displaying this amount of anger.

"She really is the bloody limit, that woman!" he said, accepting Ivan's offer of a cigarette.

"Why do we have to tolerate her?" Ivan asked. "Surely neither we nor the patients should have to put up with her rudeness."

Jim turned, looking at Ivan with a hopeless expression. "It's no good, laddie!" he said in his soft 'Geordie' accent. "She's got us by the proverbials!" Ivan winced playfully at Jim's expression. "She's a friend of Mrs Harbottle, the Hospital Management Committee chairwoman. She could make things difficult for us if we complained."

"But surely Mr Hunting knows what she's like?" Ivan said.

Jim sighed. "Oh aye, he knows all right, but he can't get Mrs H to see it. She only meets the old — er — Mrs Barton-Fanshawe at The Townswomen's Guild, where she 'queens' it in her role as Hon Sec!"

"So, what are *we* supposed to do?" Ivan asked.

"Ours is not to reason why. Ours is just to wait for the end of the shift and go to the 'Nags' to drown our sorrows!"

Ivan smiled. Jim was obviously getting back into his usual good humour. "I'd better go back into the day room," he said.

"Aye — OK!" Jim said. "If she wants me — I'm busy!"

Ivan swore good naturedly and shut the office door as he left, leaving Jim studying the racing tips in the paper. Such are the privileges of rank!

Mrs Barton-Fanshawe was leading Billy by the hand to join the group of other unfortunates that she had gathered.

"Excuse me!" Ivan said to her. "But Mr Tweedie did say that Billy shouldn't join you this evening. He has been rather disturbed of late."

She glowered at him through her pink framed reading glasses. "Young man!" she said, loftily. "I have been visiting these patients for many years now, and I think that I am a better judge of their condition than you are. Now, if you don't mind, I intend to read to them from Shakespeare. I regard their cultural education as being badly neglected by the staff of this ward!"

"Shakespeare?" Ivan said, incredulously. "Some of them can't understand the 'Beano'!"

"You are very rude!" She snorted. "I will certainly report you to Mrs Harbottle!"

"Madam!" Ivan said, trying hard to be patient. "Billy is really not well this evening, and I must ask you to leave him out for the moment."

"Certainly not!" she said. "Billy — come with me!"

She took hold of Billy's hand and led him away. Billy's reaction was to fulfil Ivan's ambition by knocking her hat flying and clawing at her throat, spilling her fake pearls all over the floor. Ivan firmly took hold of Billy's hand, preventing him from mounting a further attack. Billy, confused by what was happening, struck out, catching Ivan solidly on the jaw and knocking him to the floor. Ivan was a trifle dazed, but as he struggled to his feet, Joe leapt out of his chair and caught Billy in a bear hug, pinning him to the wall. This gave Ivan the opportunity to regain his feet. Jim came out of the office and relieved Joe of his task, leading Billy into the dormitory.

"It's all right Bill — you come to bed. You'll be OK now!"

Billy sobbed as Jim took him away.

Meanwhile, Mrs Barton-Fanshawe was trying to regain her composure as Amos, another patient, came out of the toilets. Amos had been the only survivor of a mining accident when the pit cage crashed hundreds of feet to the bottom of the mine shaft. He had been terribly injured and was now suffering from severe brain damage. Both of his legs had been shattered, leaving him with a pronounced limp. He also had a large, ugly hydrocele, a water filled hernia, which hung down almost to his knees.

One of the mental effects of Amos' brain injury was to make him rather disinhibited at times, which periodically brought the necessity of restricting his movements to the confines of the ward. As Mrs Barton-Fanshawe was on her knees frantically trying to collect her pearls, Amos smacked her playfully across her rump.

"Owdo Mrs Fat Arse!" He laughed.

"Well — really!" she spluttered. "I've never been—"

222

Before she could finish the sentence, Amos dropped his pyjama trousers, exposing the hydrocele.

"'Ow'd, you like one like this, Missus?" he grinned.

Mrs Barton-Fanshawe goggled at the sight before her eyes, then swooned into a dead faint. The floor shuddered as her massive bulk collapsed like a ton of blubber.

Jim, who had by now settled Billy down for the night, strode over to the scene of the debacle. He and Ivan lifted the prostrate form of Mrs Barton-Fanshawe and half carried-half dragged her into the office.

She quickly regained consciousness.

"Would you care for a drop of medicinal brandy?" Jim asked her.

"Well perhaps just a small one," she quavered. "It really has been a severe shock!"

"Yes, of course!" Jim tactfully agreed. He poured a stiff drink of the brandy, which was kept for just such an emergency, into a medicine glass, which he handed to Mrs Barton-Fanshawe.

She gulped it down in one, without a touch of the finesse which might have been expected of her, then thrust the glass back at Jim for a refill.

She left the ward a few minutes later, still looking somewhat dishevelled.

That, it subsequently proved, was her last visit to The Meadows. She wrote a long letter to Mrs Harbottle explaining that she felt she could no longer cope with so much responsibility, and that through the Townswomen's Guild, she had undertaken to knit a hundred bobble hats for underprivileged Eskimos.

The next afternoon, Mr Hunting brought a copy of the letter to the ward to show to the staff, mentioning that he thought Mrs Harbottle had a faint smile of relief as she handed it to him.

"It's a shame, isn't it? Poor lady!" he said, trying diplomatically not to laugh.

"Aye, it is indeed!" Jim mused, philosophically.

"I wonder if the Eskimos will write and thank her?" Ivan offered.

Both Jim and Mr Hunting collapsed into laughter. Ivan looked puzzled.

"What did I say?" he enquired, with an expression of wide-eyed innocence.

CHAPTER FOURTEEN

Ivan's allocation to his second period of night duty signified the start of his third and final year of training. Whilst he was pleased to have entered this phase of his career, he found the prospect of three months of darkness somewhat daunting. Nevertheless, he looked forward to the extra off duty days which the night shift brought as the shift was from nine p.m. to seven a.m. resulting in the forty-hour week being concluded in four shifts, rather than the six shifts of day duty each week. This meant he would be able to spend more time with Dawn.

His first night on duty was to be spent as nurse in charge of The Coppice. This was a beautiful Victorian mansion, situated towards the bottom of the hospital lane, which had been sold to the hospital board many years before, by the family who had owned it for generations, to pay off crippling death duties. The ornate, three-storied red brick building was set in three acres of magnificent grounds. The main entrance hall was oak panelled and the oak staircase had griffons and lions carved into its newel posts. Ivan had taken a liking to the old place during his first year of training, and he was looking forward to working there again.

The Coppice now served as a home for sixty elderly male patients, who, whilst they were still able to, could while away their sunset years walking and sitting in the lovely surroundings of the grounds, or enjoying the sumptuous splendour of the building. Not that all of them fully appreciated their environment!

"Aaaah! Bloody rotten owd place!" said Frank, as Ivan and his assistant for the night put him to bed.

"Don't you like it, Frank?" asked Ivan, winking at his aide.

"Ah bloody dunna!" Frank replied, his voice tinged with the disparaging tones of the chronically disgruntled. "Why couldn't they 'ave put me in a modern 'ospital?"

"Because they thought you'd like it here, Frank!" Ivan said

"Well, ah bloody dunna. An' I dunna bloody like yow neither!"

"I've always spoken very highly of you!" Ivan countered. "Why, only last night a bloke told me that you weren't fit to live with pigs, and I told him that you were!"

"Aah! An' I expect that's what yow bloody do think o' me an' all!" Frank grumbled.

"Goodnight Frank!" Ivan smiled as they left the old man's bed side.

"Bugger off!" Frank retorted, pulling the bed sheet over his head in a gesture of his withdrawal from the world.

"He's a cheerful soul, and one of nature's gentlemen!" Ivan reflected, as he and Napoleon drank their coffee once everyone was settled in bed and asleep.

"He's certainly a character!" said Nap. "But then again, so are many of us!"

"You're certainly that!" Ivan thought.

Napoleon had worked at The Meadows as a nursing assistant on night duty for many years, and stories of his many eccentricities were legion. His name was the result of an unfortunate choice by his parents, and whilst Nap did not identify himself in any way with his famous historical namesake, he did have a number of strange ideas, which, over the years, had become part of the hospital's folklore.

Ivan knew that people who are affected by certain mental illnesses often exhibit delusional tendencies. A delusion has been defined as being a false idea which is not shared by one's peers in the local community. He also knew that some delusional ideas can be of a very subtle nature. When such ideas are expressed by their progenitor, the listener often wonders if they have heard correctly, or whether the person really said what they thought had been said. Napoleon's utterances often produced this mixture if uncertainty and incredulity amongst his colleagues. His often seemingly innocuous asides could be, on further reflection, be quite shattering. As with all such human failings though, Nap's colleagues tended to mostly ignore his peculiarities in favour of his unquestionable conscientiousness and genuine concern for the welfare of his patients.

Ivan picked up the newspaper and began to read of the latest developments in the 'Cuba crisis'. Krushchev had planted missiles on the island and trained them on the USA. President Kennedy was demanding their withdrawal. American ships were stopping Soviet vessels in the Caribbean and the tension was mounting daily.

"It's a rum business!" Nap observed.

"What's that mate?" Ivan asked, lowering his paper.

"This Cuba carry on. I think it's time I did something about it!"

Ivan looked at Nap a little blankly, not being at all sure that he had just heard what he thought he'd heard. "What do you intend to do, Nap?" he asked.

"Oh, it's quite easy you know." Nap replied, nonchalantly.

"Oh yeah?"

"Well, I don't expect you to believe me!" Nap sniffed. "But I'll show you how it's done if you like!"

"How what's done?" Ivan felt compelled to ask, wondering what he was letting himself in for.

Nap went to the desk and took out a piece of paper, which he tore into four one-inch squares. He wrote the name of various capital cities on each square. London, Moscow, Paris, Washington DC were all allocated to a square.

"What's the capital of Cuba?" he asked.

Ivan thought for a moment. "Havana?" he offered.

"Hmmm!" Nap mused. He wrote 'Havana' on one square and added it to the others. Having done so, he wrapped all the squares of paper in a handkerchief and stuffed the lot down the back of his trousers. Grimacing, he contorted his face, blowing out his cheeks and clenching his jaw. Suddenly, he broke wind, so loudly that Ivan visibly started.

"Beg pardon!" Nap said. "It's the pressure you know?"

"Yes, I suppose it must be," Ivan babbled, wondering what to expect next.

"Well, that's it!" said Nap. "Can't do any more tonight! They'll just have to sort it out amongst themselves. More coffee?"

Ivan handed his cup to Nap, not knowing whether to be concerned or amused at what he had just witnessed. He was certainly perplexed and remained so for the rest of the night shift, although Nap's conversation from then on was relatively normal.

The following evening, Ivan entered the Charge Nurse's office to find the holder of that title, Tom Henson, talking to Nap.

"Hello mate!" said Nap. "Have you read the paper yet?"

"No, I slept fairly well today, and I haven't been up for long," Ivan replied. "Why? Have you won the pools?"

Nap handed him *The Daily Mirror*. "Here — have a look at this!" he said.

Ivan took the paper and looked at the front-page headlines. It appeared that Comrade Krushchev had backed down and removed the missiles. The paper showed a jubilant President Kennedy, pictured shortly after receiving the news.

Nap left the room and Ivan turned to Tom. "Do you realise that the world has just been saved by a fart?" he asked.

"You've been workin' wi' that daft bugger too long!" Tom grunted. "G'night!" Tom left the building!

Carlo was an Italian nursing assistant, who, because Italians in the 1960s were still registered as 'aliens', had been steered into nursing by the British government, as nursing was one of the reserved occupations for natives of those countries which had opposed Britain during the Second World War. He was, by trade, a carpenter, and a very good one, as several very nicely made coffee tables which graced the homes of various staff members would bear witness to. Whilst Carlo accepted the necessity of his enforced change of occupation, he longed for the day when after the prescribed number of years of residence in the UK, he could return to his true vocation. As a son of the beautiful city of Sorrento, the home of excellent inlaid furniture, he hoped to establish a business within these shores. As a result of this predicament, he was never likely to rise to the top of the nursing profession, but despite his very fractured English, he did his best, and was well thought of by his colleagues. He had been on permanent night duty for two years now, having spent his first two years working around the male wards on day duty. In the process, he had acquired a turn of phrase not unlike Chico Marx, and this afforded much amusement to his colleagues.

Ivan found difficulty in suppressing a grin when Carlo described the televised match of the previous evening between Manchester United and

Napoli. "I-a-tell you, we were magnifico!" he said, with much gesticulation. "If-a-da ref 'ad-a-sent off — a-creep Bobby Charlton, we'd-a-won easy!"

"What did Bobby Charlton ever do to get sent off for?" Ivan asked, amazed at the very suggestion.

"When-a-da Napoli backs-a-try a to stop heem, he run-a-too fast. Da Napoli fella he fall-a-down. He lie on-a-da ground. He clutch-a-da leg and-a-scream and shout. Da ref, he-a-take-a-no notice. I-a-tell-a-you, dat Charlton, he is-a-da butcher. He might 'ave killed-a-da Napoli boy!"

"Perhaps the ref thought it was not quite cricket?" Ivan suggested.

"Wha' da ya mean? Issa no creeket. Dey play-a-da football, no?"

"Wha da ya mean, wha da I mean-a? Ivan said, warming to his subject.

Carlo bristled. "Wha-da-ya talking like-a dat for? Are you-a-takin'-a-da piss?"

"No, I'm-a-no-takin'-a-da piss!" Ivan said. "Blimey, you've got me at it now. Go and do the last round!"

The 'round', as it was known, was the patrolling of four wards which were not staffed overnight. It was the least liked job for the night staff. It was this individual's responsibility to walk thorough each ward every hour, checking for clandestine Woodbine smokers, who could present a fire risk, and generally just ensuring that all was as it should be. He would then return to Male Twelve to act as 'second' to the nurse in charge. Whilst this system was economical on staff allocation, saving at least three nurses who would mainly have to sit all night listening to the patients snoring, it was impossible for the roundsman to be in four places simultaneously, thereby creating a slight degree of risk.

Carlo left Male Twelve at five-forty-five a.m. to walk around his four wards for the penultimate time. He would go round again at seven a.m. at the end of the night shift to hand over to the day Charge Nurses. To Ivan's surprise, he was back ten minutes later.

"Have you been right round?" Ivan asked him.

"Sure! Dey all-a-sleep like-a-da babies!" he said.

Ivan looked concerned. "But have you checked each patient to see if they are all OK?"

"Whaddya mean 'OK'?" he asked.

"Just make sure that they are breathing!" Ivan said. "There's no need to wake them if they're still asleep, but check particularly on the ones who sleep in the side rooms. They tend to get missed!"

Carlo's face took on a look of surprise and trepidation. "Hey! Why you say 'alive and breathing' like-a-dat?"

Ivan began to get a little angry with him. "Because it has been known for old men to wake up dead, and the shock often kills them! Now do as I say and check round again, properly!"

Carlo set off again without much enthusiasm. Ivan's little outburst, although partly humorous, had obviously rattled him, and he muttered darkly as he went. Ivan turned his attention to the patients of Male Twelve who were beginning to stir.

Five minutes later, the phone rang. "Male Twelve, Reader!" Ivan answered.

A stream of frantic Italian gibberish emanated from the receiver. "Hold on, Carlo!" he said. "What's the matter?"

"He's-a-dead! He's-a-dead!" Carlo screamed.

"Whos'-a-dead? I mean-who's dead?"

He's-dead-he's a dead! Madre Mia! Whad am I-a-gonna do?" Carlo howled.

"Tell me where you are!" Ivan shouted back.

Carlo ranted on in Italian for thirty seconds, then the line went dead.

Ivan thought for a moment, then dialled the office of Wally Brown, the night superintendent.

"It's Carlo!" he said, as Wally answered. "He's found a patient dead on the round, but I don't know which ward he's in!"

"OK, I'll go and look for him," Wally said.

A few minutes later, the door opened and Wally came in, supporting a tottering Carlo.

"He'll be OK in a few minutes!" Wally said. "He's had a bit of a fright. He looked at Billy Bloor in the dark! I'll go and finish the round for him!"

At the mention of Billy's name, realisation came to Ivan like a bolt from the blue. Billy was a sprightly old man of eighty-five who suffered from chronic anaemia. He also suffered from insomnia, and was prescribed a fairly large dose of Sodium Amytal to help him to sleep. Ivan had once been caught out by Billy in this state, and he now found that he had some sympathy with Carlo's state of shock. Sodium Amytal is a barbiturate drug, and because of the unpleasant side effects of this type of medication, it has since been replaced by more modern, less potent preparations.

One of the problems associated with the barbiturates is that they tend to depress the respiratory centre of the brain. This can produce a characteristically long pause between inhalation and expiration — 'nocturnal apnoea'. Carlo, looking at Billy's white, immobile face and noticing that he was not breathing, assumed that the worst had happened. He had returned to the bedside after the one-sided telephone call to Ivan when the 'corpse' suddenly sat up, yawned and stretched. It was at this point in time that Wally had entered the ward from behind Carlo, tapping the terror-struck Italian on the shoulder. In his highly charged, nervous state, Carlo screamed loudly, waking up all the patients who were still asleep. It took Wally a few minutes to settle them all down again, during which time Carlo fell to his knees to pray for his salvation.

Ivan went on duty the following night and was met in the ward office by a bright and breezy Carlo, apparently fully recovered from his ordeal.

"How are you feeling?" Ivan asked him.

"I'm-a-feelin' OK!" Carlo said, nonchalantly.

"You're quite sure?"

"Sure, I'm-a-sure!" Carlo said. "Why-a-ask? Do you think I'm-a-crazy?"

"Not at all!" Ivan assured him. "But you did have a pretty nasty shock!"

Carlo shrugged, dismissively. "Ah! It would-a-take-a-more than that to frighten Carlo!"

He set off on his rounds. That night, each round took him an hour to complete!

CHAPTER FIFTEEN

As Ivan's three-year training period drew inexorably towards its culmination in the final state examination, he found that his ability to assess the patient's symptoms and form a diagnosis in his own mind was increasing.

Very often, Ivan's 'private' diagnosis of a patient who was either newly admitted or previously unknown to him tallied very closely with the more precise, carefully considered diagnosis arrived at by the medical staff. This 'rule of thumb' technique was not encouraged by the nursing tutors, who held that it was no part of a nurse's role to formulate a diagnosis. Nevertheless, Ivan considered himself to be a fairly competent judge of these matters. His confidence, however, was about to be badly shaken by the coming of George.

Ivan was now back on day duty on Male Reception, the 'admission' ward. George was brought in by the police in the early hours of the morning, after they had arrested him for driving under the influence of alcohol or drugs.

George was himself a doctor — a general practitioner — who's practice was situated in one of the most fashionable parts of the county. He had been uncooperative towards the police when they stopped his car, which they considered was being erratically driven. This led to him being taken back to the police station under arrest. He appeared before the magistrates the following day, and as result of the incoherence of George's responses to questions, he was placed on a probation order which warranted his detention under the appropriate section of the mental health act for psychiatric reports. These reports would eventually be placed before the court, guiding the decision as to what, if any, sentence should be awarded.

"They're always difficult patients!" Bob Bracewell's apparently bigoted attitude surprised Ivan, as he had always regarded Bob with considerable respect.

"Who are?" Ivan asked, eyebrows raised.

"Doctors! You mark my words — he'll moan and complain like anything when he's been here for a day or two!"

After a little more thought on the subject, Ivan decided that Bob may be having an 'off' day, so he put the incident out of mind for the time being.

In mid-morning, Ivan attended the clinical conference which Dr O' Riley, the new

Consultant Psychiatrist had called. The doctor's intention was to get all the staff who had contact with his patients — doctors, nurses, Occupational Therapists, Psycholgists etcetera, together at regular intervals to discuss and co-ordinate their views on the patients' progress. By doing so, he had created a therapeutic team which would bring all the skills and knowledge of the various staff groups to bear on the patients' problems. This had proved to be eminently successful, and Ivan enjoyed attending the meetings.

"Now, we turn our attention to the case of Dr George Fairburn," Dr O' Riley announced, as opened the patient's file in front of him.

"As I expect you all know, the patient originally presented with a history of drug abuse, which he has always insisted came about as a result of his attempts at self-medication, in an effort to find some relief from his underlying depression. Unfortunately, he became increasingly reliant upon the amphetamines, and this resulted in his 'brush with the law'. His problems have increased manifoldly since this incident, and he now faces, in addition to his previous difficulties, the prospect of disciplinary action being taken against him by both his employers and the General Medical Council."

"I am sure I do not need to spell out to any of you the possible catastrophic effects which this situation could result in for a patient who is already in an extremely vulnerable and sensitive position. I would particularly ask you all to be very carefully and meticulously observant whenever you are dealing with him during this phase of his life."

At the end of the conference, and at Bob's request, Ivan went into the day room and sat by George, who turned his attention from the TV to smile weakly, in acknowledgment of Ivan's presence.

"What was the verdict then?" he asked, guessing that he had been the subject of discussion at the conference. "Am I to plead 'guilty but insane' or will I be thrown into some dungeon and left to rot?"

He grinned quizzically, anticipating Ivan's slight discomfiture at his question, and seeming to take some pleasure from this.

"Well, you certainly earned the honour of being this week's prize conundrum!" Ivan said, attempting to inject a little levity into the proceedings. "We may enter you for the 'medical mystery of the month' award in *Doctors Weekly*!"

To Ivan's relief, George laughed at this. "It never was difficult to confuse an Irishman!" he grinned, obviously referring to Dr O' Riley. "Let's face it. If I can't fathom it out, he's got no chance!"

"Physician, heal thyself, eh?" Ivan offered.

"Something like that, I suppose. My training tells me that I can't start the healing process without a diagnosis, and I've been wondering what's wrong with myself for the past five years or so. It's only comparatively recently that I have had any clues at all as to what besets my tortured psyche!"

"Do you mean that you think you know what's wrong?" Ivan asked.

"I mean that I think I know what I think I know, but maybe I don't know at all!" George said, turning his attention back to the TV, thereby signalling to Ivan that he wished to end the discussion.

Ivan left him watching a cartoon, noting as he did so that George did not show the faintest trace of amusement at the antics of the cartoon characters, whilst many of the others in the room were in guffaws.

The following day, George asked Ivan for the key to the bathroom. As he had done on previous occasions, he was quick to pick up Ivan's repressed questioning look.

"It's all right!" he said. "I have no intention of drowning myself whilst on hospital property!" he said, sardonically.

"No intention, perhaps, but you could do it by accident!" Ivan replied.

"If the rules of the game require you to play voyeur whilst I attend to my personal hygiene, then so be it!" George answered.

"I assure you that I'm only doing this because I get paid for it!" Ivan said, trying once more to bring some jocularity to the proceedings. "I lost my amateur status years ago!"

George began to undress whilst Ivan ran water into the bath. He eventually turned and straightened to find George regarding him with a perplexed expression. "Seriously though, why do you do this job?"

"Why do you ask?" Ivan returned.

"I would have thought that a chap like you would have found it difficult to come to terms with at times."

"Not particularly," Ivan said. Why do you qualify your question with 'a chap like you'?"

"Well, before I came in here on the wrong side of the fence, so to speak, I had limited experience of working with male nurses. I must say that you blokes don't fit the image I had previously had in my mind! I just wondered what attracted apparently normal young men like yourself and your colleagues into this walk of life?"

"What you are trying to say is that you thought we would all be poofs!" Ivan said, trying hard to conceal his irritation.

"I don't know what I expected," George said. "But whatever I did expect, none of you seem to be 'it'!"

"Ah! Who amongst us is what he seems to be?" Ivan quoted.

"Touché!" said George. "I suppose that I should be the last person to find another world on the other side of the looking glass, where nothing is quite the way that one had expected it to be. After all, if I were playing my present game according to 'the rules', I should have a whole set of neurotic 'hang ups' centred around my personal identity crisis. As it is though, I don't, because I have no doubts about either who I am or what I want to be! I freely admit that my knowledge of psychiatry was gained as a member of a somewhat disinterested group of medical students. We had a series of not overly helpful lectures on the subject, but I am somewhat puzzled by my feelings of depression when there doesn't appear to be an exogenous cause."

"Perhaps the cause is endogenous then?" Ivan suggested, as George lowered himself into the bath.

"The Irishman doesn't think so," he said. "At least, he tells me that I don't display the usual set of signs and symptoms."

"Are there any unusual ones then?" Ivan asked.

"How do you mean?" George asked.

Ivan found a stool and sat down by George's left shoulder, attempting to lessen the impression that he was 'on guard'. "I mean, are there any factors that you are reluctant to mention, but which could be significant?"

"Well, there are one or two items I've thought of running past the O' Riley to see what his reaction was, but I haven't done it so far?"

"What not?" Ivan asked.

"It's difficult. I know that I may seem to be a little critical of Dr O' Riley, but the man is no fool, and I don't want to appear to be 'pulling rank'."

"You mean that you find it difficult to forget your own medical background and simply put yourself into Dr O' Riley's hands?"

"Something like that!" George said.

"I see," Ivan said. "Well, nothing ventured, nothing gained. Why don't you try your theories out on me first? Then, if I don't collapse into hysterics at the absurdity, it may be worth taking to a higher court?"

"OK!" George said. "You asked for it!" He stood up in the bath and pointed to a large scar on his abdomen. "See this?"

Ivan looked a little more closely. "Don't tell me!" he said. "It looks like the result of an appendicectomy that was carried out with a pair of garden shears rather than a scalpel!"

"You're nearly right!" George replied. "It's actually the hole where a piece of North Korean shrapnel entered my life, my gut and my spleen, and various other bits and pieces. It was quite a mess at the time. Took the army surgeons about nine hours to reassemble me!"

"Yes — very nasty!" said Ivan. "So, how does that connect with the subject under discussion?"

George continued with his ablutions. "While they were sorting out which bits were mine and which were North Korea's, they resected about two and a half yards of my small intestine. That is, they removed it from the plumbing altogether. I remember this Lieutenant Colonel — 'Bart's' man in Civvy Street — telling me that I'd get along fine with an abbreviated gut, and that the only trouble I was likely to have would be excessive flatulence! He laughed at that — thought it was hilarious, the pompous bastard. Looked right down on we ordinary mortals who did our medical training in the provinces. I remember thinking at the time that I'd love to prove him wrong. Well, now, I think I may have done so!"

"How do you mean?" Ivan asked.

George climbed out of the bath and reached for the towel which Ivan offered to him. "Think about the physiology that goes on in the small bowel."

Ivan searched his memory for what he'd learned on this subject. "Absorption of water, some minerals and fats!" he muttered, half to himself and half to George.

"And?"

"Vitamins!" Ivan said, after a little more thought.

"Hooray!" said George. "Go to the top of the class! Particularly, young man — the B complex, deficiency of which is well known for causing Beri Beri, mental disturbances and spots on the dickie!"

"And you think you're short of one of the B complex?" Ivan suggested.

"I don't just think I am — I've proved it! I sent some of my own blood off to the lab, with a fictious patient's name on it, and it came back showing lowered levels of B12 and folates. So, over a period of several years, who knows?" He began to dress.

"Have you voiced this to Dr O' Riley yet?"

George smiled, wanly. "Not yet. I thought I'd try it out on a few if you blokes first to see if any of you fell about laughing!".

Ivan handed George his socks. "So, what you mean is, that you'd like us to suggest it to the good doctor and pretend that it was our idea. That way, if he laughs it out of the door, your integrity remains intact!"

George looked at him intensely. "Would you do that?"

"Not me!" Ivan said. "I'm too lowly — but Bob might do it?"

George looked pensive. "Can you sell it to him?"

"I'll give it a try," said Ivan. "If I win, and if he sells it to Dr O' Riley — what then?"

George smiled. "Ah! What indeed?" George mused. "Then, perhaps, you'll have helped one of your wretched charges to a happier old age!" Ivan threw a wet sponge at him, in jest, as he went out of the bathroom door.

Ivan found Bob alone in the office later that morning. He did his best to introduce George's theory as tactfully as he could, but the look on Bob's face told him that the Charge Nurse was sceptical.

"I told you — doctors as psychiatric patients are bad news!" Bob said. "They always try to ascribe their problems to some extraneous factor, rather than face up to the possibility that they may be personally lacking in some way. I think it's due to the myth of medical infallibility."

"So, you think it's a myth, do you?" Ivan grinned.

Bob smiled grimly. "When you've seen them cock up as many times as I have, you'll know it's a myth!"

"Do you think he might have a point though"? Ivan asked.

"He might have, and pigs might fly. Go and help Harry with the medicines, will you?" Bob brought the conversation to an end by turning to his paperwork.

A few days later, Ivan met George coming out of Dr O' Riley's consulting room.

"Ah! Just the chap I wanted to see!" George said.

"So, what does he think of your idea?"

George smiled — the first time Ivan had seen him really do so. "Someone had already suggested it to him. He's putting me on Vitamin B12 injections!"

A few weeks later, Dr O' Riley sanctioned George's discharge from hospital. Ivan and Bob waved him off as he got into his wife's car for the journey home.

Ivan turned to Bob. "Well, it looks as though he was right!"

Bob grinned. "You know what they say — a bit of what you fancy does you good!"

CHAPTER SIXTEEN

Jock and Vic sat at the breakfast table in the staff dining room as Ivan joined them for his breakfast break. It had always struck Ivan as being a little odd that the staff should commence duty at seven a.m. then be allowed to take a thirty-minute break after working for only one to one to one and a half hours. As with many other features of life in a mental hospital at that time, the origins of the practice were lost in a welter of tradition. Joe Joiner had once expressed the opinion that in the good old — bad old days long ago, when the staff were known as 'attendants' rather than 'nurses', a good breakfast was essential if they were to stand up to the frequent physical struggles required to restrain disturbed patients, when in the days before violent behaviour was controlled by medication.

This line of thought, if carried on into conversation, invariably led to a long and usually unresolved discussion on the relative values and efficacies of the major tranquilisers against the need to prevent physical aggression by other means. As a result, the subject was not discussed as frequently as perhaps it should have been, and certainly not over breakfast on a grey October morning.

Ivan sat down and sliced the top off his boiled egg, whilst regarding his two companions with the appropriate detachment for the early hour of day. Vic was reading the newspaper, whilst Jock was engrossed in an article in a nursing magazine.

"Good morning, Ivan!" he said to himself. "And how are we today? Isn't it pleasant to be in the company of two old and close friends, at a time when the three of us are approaching the apex of our careers, the culmination of our ambitions and the possible realisation of our dreams of becoming fully fledged pillars of society, persons who will command the respect and admiration of our community for their selfless dedication to duty and their hard-earned expertise in the ancient and novel art of healing?"

"What are you going on about?" Vic grunted from behind his newspaper.

"Aye — whisht mon. Ye're putting me off ma porridge!" Jock skirled, in his broadest Aberdonian accent.

Ivan addressed them again. "What I was trying to remind you of, gentlemen, is the inescapable and inexorable approach of the state final examination in three weeks' time. It may have escaped your attention, but we have all been so preoccupied with our extra mural activities of late, that we have done little, if any, studying or revision."

"Aaach awa wi' ye!" Jock drawled. "It's not that close!" Then — realisation dawned! "Three weeks did ye say?"

"Three weeks!" yelled Vic, dropping the newspaper. "I haven't looked at a book for months!"

"Aye — now ye mention it — neither have I!" Jock said, echoing Vic's note of panic.

Ivan noted their troubled countenances.

Ivan realised that they were both looking at him with mixed expressions of panic, despair and apprehension.

"Well — don't look at me!" he said. "I'm no further forward than you two are. We'd better get down to some work at nights instead of wasting our time boozing and indulging in pleasures of the flesh!"

"Speak for yourself!" chortled Vic. "Anyway, who said those things are a waste of time?"

"Far be it from me!" Ivan said, with an air of wounded innocence. "But seriously though, I do think that perhaps we ought to be making an effort."

There followed a period of intense nocturnal activity, as the three friends tried to cram three years' revision into three weeks. They had covered the entire curriculum of subjects laid down by the General Nursing Council in their syllabus for the Certificate in Mental Nursing, possession of which made them eligible for inclusion on the Register of Nurses, in their studies and lectures in the School of Nursing under Ted Jones' tutelage. All too frequently, however, they would come to realise that attending a lecture on a subject, allied to a little reading on the matter, did not automatically confer upon them the depth of understanding that they were now acutely conscious of lacking. As the date of the examination drew unrelentingly nearer, their respective moods and emotions traversed between feelings of relative calm and quiet confidence through uncomfortable nagging doubts to total amnesia provoking blind panic. Ivan recalled Ted's words during one of his lectures on anxiety neurosis, which were:

"It is very difficult for those who have never suffered a mental illness to truly empathise with those who have. You will, however, have a golden opportunity to study the symptoms of anxiety neurosis when you come to sit your 'finals'! Note the sweating palms, the dryness of the mouth, the churning of the abdominal viscera. Observe the feelings of panic, naked terror and helplessness. Try to imagine what it must be like to feel like that every day of your life. But you make take some comfort in the knowledge that you can at least ascribe your own wretchedness to your guilt and remorse over wasted time and lost opportunity in keeping up with your studies. Those who are pathologically ill, do not have that ability. But if you really are worried at this stage, just think of all the bloody idiots who you have worked with in the past who have passed their exams. This may bring you some comfort!"

A few nights before the date of the examination, Ivan decided to relieve the pressure by taking Dawn out for a drink at their favourite country pub. They had often sat in the garden of the inn watching the summer sun set over the distant hills, with the warm evening breezes carrying the scent of mown hay, or wood smoke from a distant bonfire, as the swifts and swallows swooped low in pursuit of their miniscule prey. On this autumn evening, however, they sat in wooden armchairs and bathed in the warm glow of burning logs in the ingle nook. They had often sat there, not talking, but merely holding hands, content with each other's company, as they did on this particular evening. It was Dawn who broke the silence.

"What will you do after you've passed your exam?" she asked.

Ivan thought for a while. "I haven't actually given the matter a lot of thought," he said. "I suppose I'll stay at The Meadows for a while as a Staff Nurse. I'll need a couple of years at that level before I'm a candidate for promotion."

Dawn smiled. "I know that, silly! No, I meant what were you intending to do after that time? I expect that Jock will be looking for a job in Scotland, and I know that Vic would like to go abroad. I wondered what you would like to do?"

Ivan looked puzzled. "Well, that's a maybe for those two, but I thought you knew that I have no real urge to wander, at least, not at the moment. Besides, we'll have to find a place to live, and our chances of a council flat will be better around here than anywhere else."

"Oh! So, you're thinking of settling down with someone, are you?" she asked, distractedly playing with the olive on a stick in her drink.

Ivan looked at her incredulously. "What are you talking about?"

"I'm talking about you finding somewhere to live. You used the word 'we'! I just wondered who the other party might be?"

Ivan was even more puzzled now. "What do you mean by 'the other party'!" he asked.

"I mean who are you going to live with?" She sipped her drink, eyeing him impishly.

Ivan gaped, mystified by this turn in the conversation. "Why, with you of course! Who else?"

"With me?" she whooped, pointing at herself. "Oh, I don't think that would be a good idea! I mean, what would the neighbours think? And what about my mother and all the people we work with. What would they be saying?"

"What's it got to do with them?" he asked, looking a little flushed. He was feeling both a little angry and alarmed at Dawn's attitude.

"Well!" she said. "I don't suppose it would really have anything to do with the neighbours, and the people at work would eventually find something else to talk about, but I can't see my mother ever coming to terms with it. No, I'm sorry Ivan, but it won't work!" She reached for her coat.

"Where are you going?" he asked, stunned.

"I'd be grateful if you'd take me home." She sniffed. "I'm feeling a bit upset."

He looked desperate. "Just a minute. Sit down and let's try and sort all this out." She hesitated for a few seconds and then sat down. "That's better!" he said, in a placatory tone. He took her hand, which she did not attempt to prevent. "Now then." he said. "What's upset you? What did I say?"

She dabbed her nose with a frilly little handkerchief which she had pulled from her handbag. "It was just that it came as a bit of a shock — are you suggesting that we should live together. I perhaps wouldn't have minded if you hadn't taken it for granted, but you did, didn't you?" She began to look a little more composed.

Ivan was perplexed. "But I always thought that your Mum liked me? We always seem to get on well and can have a bit of a laugh!"

"Oh!" said Dawn. "She does like you, but I'm still not sure what she'd think about us living in sin. I think she has always assumed that we would get married first. She's a bit old fashioned like that!"

Ivan's look of incredulity was growing by the minute. "What are you going on about?" he asked. "I'm not asking you to live in sin with me!"

She turned. "You're not?"

"Of course not. What made you think that I was?"

"Well!" she began. "What else then?"

"What else?" he asked, raising his voice a little. "We'll be married, of course!"

"Will we?" She breathed. "I didn't realise that was what you meant!"

"You amaze me!" he said. "It's always been understood that we'd get married after I have passed my finals. You can carry on with your studies after we're married, but we wouldn't have managed on student's pay!"

She looked at him, her lips twitching into a long-repressed smile, which quicky developed into a fit of uncontrolled giggling. "I wish you could have seen your face!" she said. She sat back in the chair, convulsed with laughter.

"I'll never understand women!" Ivan said. "One minute you're crying, and then—"

Dawn regained a modicum of composure. "I agree that it's always been understood we'd be married after you qualified, but you've never actually asked me, you know?"

Ivan's mouth opened and closed soundlessly, as he fought for the words to say. "You mean, er, that is, I never, but I'm sure—"

She stood her ground. "You never asked me!"

Ivan frantically tried to collect his scrambled wits. This was a serious situation, which called for a suitably adroit remedy.

Suddenly, to Dawn's utter astonishment, he leapt onto a chair. "Ladies and gentlemen!" he cried. "May I have your attention please?"

A sudden hush fell over the crowd. All eyes turned in the couple's direction. Dawn looked as though she was about to flee the room, but before she could do so, Ivan spoke again. "Friends!" he began, to a background of titters and giggles. "Some of you here tonight may know me, and some may not! Indeed, upon looking round the room, I see that some of you are unfortunate enough to number me amongst your colleagues, whilst some of you have been even more cruelly treated by fate as to be amongst my personal friends."

Dawn was flushed with embarrassment. "Get down, you idiot!" she said. "You're showing me up!"

Ivan looked down upon her from his lofty and somewhat shaky perch. "Ah, Madam!" He spoke in Shakespearian tones. "One so beautiful should insist on being shown up. The whole world should see your beauty, and worship at your door!"

"I'll kill you!" Dawn hissed, through clenched teeth.

"Friends!" Ivan continued. "You see before you a man consumed by passion, and yet also transfixed by guilt—"

"More like sloshed in bitter ale!" some wag shouted from the far end of the room, drawing laughter from the crowd.

Ivan let the laughter die away, taking his timing from the audience like a professional comedian.

"Ah friends! You may scoff!" he said. "But I must call on all of you to act as witnesses to my public correction of a terrible wrong that I have wrought!" He covered his eyes in mock wretchedness.

"Boo! Gerroff! Scrag 'Im!" yelled his pals, rising to the occasion.

"Nay my friends! Do not mock a soul in torment! I have been guilty of a heinous lack of valour, the foulest of all slights to a woman! Yes, my friends, I have taken the beautiful young lady before you for granted. I have presumed upon her affection in such foolhardy manner that I falsely assumed that she would grant me her hand in marriage. Now, I am bereft!"

"You're pissed!" shouted the voice from the back.

"That too!" Ivan agreed to the delight of the throng. "Such is my shame that the only recourse open to me is to right this dreadful wrong here and now, in the sight of this gathering!"

He jumped down from the chair and knelt at Dawn's feet. "Dawn!" he said, looking up at her like a worshipper at the feet of a goddess. "Will you do me the ultimate and wondrous honour of becoming my wife? Say yes and save me from this torment!"

Dawn, who had now almost recovered her cool, smiled. "I will!" she said. The crowd whistled and hooted their approval. "But only on one condition!"

"Name it, my treasure!" Ivan said, drawing further gales of laughter.

Dawn stood up. "Promise me now, before these good citizens, that you will never again eat pickled onions in bed!"

"For your hand, my love, I would crawl bare arsed to London. Be mine, and I'll buy your mother a new anvil for her smithy!"

Dawn threw her arms around him, helpless with laughter. The landlord, who had witnessed the whole extraordinary affair from behind the bar, brought out a small bottle of champagne, with his compliments.

"Thanks very much!" Ivan said.

"S' all right!" said the landlord. "I'd like to book the pair of you as a cabaret act!"

News of the betrothal reached the ears of Jock and Vic the following day.

"Lucky sod!" Vic grunted over the breakfast table. "How can a nice girl like that waste herself on a berk like him?" He jerked his thumb at Ivan, winking at Jock as he did so.

"Aye, she's a braw lassie!" Jock burred. "Ma heart fair bleeds at the thought o' the poor, wee hen ha'eing to wash his socks!"

"Thanks friends!" Ivan said. "But seriously though, this whole business gives me a problem!"

"He thinks he's got problems now!" Vic said. "Wait until he's got six kids round his ankles. *then* he'll really have problems!"

"Shurupp!" Ivan said. "The problem is that as you are both foolish enough to allow yourself to

260

be classed as my closest friends, I can't decide on which one of you to ask to be my best man!"

"That's easy," Jock said.

Ivan's brow creased. "It is?"

"Aye!" said Jock. "Ask Bob Bracewell. We'll be your ushers!"

"Blast!" said Ivan, looking up at his Caledonian friend.

"What's up wi' ye the noo?" asked Jock.

"I was hoping you'd wear your kilt and be the chief bridesmaid!" He ducked as Jock threw a bread roll at his head.

The marriage of a nurse always creates something of a problem in any hospital. The bride-to-be will need time off for the fitting of the dress, to attend rehearsals for the service and to visit the Vicar for that 'frank and earnest' little talk which is dispensed to all who are about to tie the knot. Whilst it is true that the bride-to-be will have the normal time off duty available to her, it never seems to fit in with the thousand and one bits of business which are essential to the prenuptial preparations. Add to that the double difficulty if both participants in the wedding are members of the staff of the same hospital, and it easy to see why, in bygone ages, most nurses were also nuns!

After Ivan and Dawn had paid their somewhat nervous visits to Mr Hunting and the Matron to arrange their duties to allow for all the appointments for the aforementioned bits of business, they were relatively free to go ahead with the main arrangements for the wedding. Only one thing now stood between the happy couple and a life of marital bliss — *the final exams*!

"It's all right for you pair!" Ivan muttered into his beer. "It's not as important if you pass or fail. If I 'dip', we can't afford to get married."

Vic looked at Jock, his expression conveying volumes. "Think so, eh? Well, let me tell you something Sunshine! I've already had the offer of a tidy little job in Cornwall if I pass, and Haggis here has, this very morning, received all the details of 'how to go to Australia' for ten quid. So, don't run away with the idea that you're the only one who's dreams could be shattered by the arrival of the dreaded brown envelope. If I don't spend a few summers in the good Cornish air, the flower of my youth will wilt before it's dropped its first petal, and if Jock doesn't get out of the country before that bird from Glasgow's dad catches up with him, we'll have a vacancy for a mate. In short — buck up, look on the bright side, have faith in your innate ability to charm the examiners into letting you through and cough up — it's your round!"

Ivan feigned a deliberately missed punch at his mate's grinning countenance and made for the bar with the empty glasses. On his return, he looked pensively at his two friends. "So! This is it!" he said.

"This is what?" Jock asked rhetorically.

"The impending end of our long and happy relationship," Ivan said, wistfully.

"Aye, I suppose that's true," said the Scot. "I hadnae thought o' it like that. Sad, isn't it? But just remember, laddie. Before ye and Vic here wave me away damp eyed at the airport — I lent ye a fiver twa years ago. I'll no get on the plane wi'out it!"

"I didn't know you wanted to emigrate until Vic just mentioned it." Ivan said. "When did you decide on that?"

"I told you, when that big Glaswegian bloke started looking for the cause of his daughter's fall from grace!" Vic laughed.

Jock looked disdainful. "Awa' wi' ye're nonsense!" he skirled. "I dinnae know any lassie from Glasgie." He turned to Ivan. "I've been making inquiries for some time the noo, but ye've bin so tied up wi' love's young dream, ye didna see!"

"Bad for the eyesight, this stardust!" said Vic. "Have you asked Bob yet?"

"Yes!" Ivan replied. "He said he'd do it if the price was right. When I asked him to submit a tender, he said he'd ring the railway and hire one. I sometimes fear for his sanity!"

"Let's face it!" said Vic. "If he's worked with the three of us, it's no wonder he's cracking under the strain. Ah! Speak of the devil!"

Bob Bracewell walked over to the three of them having collected his pint from the bar. "This is no way to revise for the exam," he joked.

"We're studying the effects of alcohol on the free will," said Ivan. "Every time Jock pays for the beer, we know he's weakening!"

"Well, it won't be long now until you're all under the watchful eye of the invigilator. The written part was the easy bit for me. I fell apart during the practical. I took a tray of instruments out of the steriliser and dropped the bloody lot at the feet of the examiner. I must have done something right though, as I passed first time. Have you bought the ring yet?" he asked Ivan.

"Got it today! It's a big chunky thing with milled edges."

"Sounds like my mother-in-law!" Said Bob He downed his beer. "Well, come on you lot. We may as well walk back down the lane together. It's a big day tomorrow!"

CHAPTER SEVENTEEN

"Have you all got your examination cards?" Ted Jones asked the candidates, as they waited nervously outside the exam room. Ivan felt inside his pocket for the umpteenth time that morning and was reassured by the feel of the envelope that contained the card.

"Remember, you will not be permitted to sit the exam without the card as proof that you are who you claim to be. You will be told by the invigilator to write your examination number in the space provided for it at the top left corner of the answer book. That number is the only means by which the examiner who marks your paper will identify you. They are not told your name or which hospital you are from. You're just a number to him or her, so it's no use trying to bribe them!"

The anxious candidates laughed at Ted's jocularity, grateful for the slight easing of the tense atmosphere which the occasion gave rise to. Ivan felt himself gulp slightly as the door of the exam room opened at the precise stroke of nine a.m.

The twenty or so candidates filed into the room and were ushered to their individual desks by the grim-faced invigilator. This lady gave the impression to Ivan that she was one of the 'skinny lipped virgins with blood like water' soliloquised in the musical 'Oklahoma!'.

When the candidates were all seated, she took her position at the front of the room.

She nodded to Ted, who was at the back of the room, and he stepped forward carrying the sealed parcel of exam papers bearing the insignia of the General Nursing Council for England and Wales, placing it on the table in front of the invigilator, who broke the seal and lifted out the papers. These papers bore the questions, which until that moment had been a closely guarded secret, to be answered by the candidates. The answers provided by each entrant were to be written in the special foolscap-sized answer books which had been already placed on the desks. The papers were distributed by Ted, who then withdrew from the room.

The invigilator peered at her tiny wristwatch.

"Very well, ladies and er gentlemen," she said, fixing Ivan, Vic and Jock, the only male candidates, with a baleful glare.

"The time is now ten past nine, and the examination will commence at nine fifteen precisely. Please do not open your question papers until I tell you to do so. You must attempt to answer six of the ten questions therein, and you will have three hours in which to do so. If any of you wish to leave the room during the examination, you must be accompanied by myself or one of the assistant invigilators who are stationed outside the door. If you have finished all your answers before the three hours have elapsed, you may quietly leave after handing your answer book to me. Failure to comply with these rules will render you liable to disqualification from today's examination, and if you should be disqualified, I am obliged to destroy your paper and report the matter to council. Any evidence of cheating, copying from other candidates or reading from pre-prepared notes will, if I am satisfied by the evidence, also cause your disqualification. May I ask you now, please, to write your examination numbers on your answer papers."

There was a rustling of papers, scratching of pens and an outbreak of nervous coughs and giggles which were quickly silenced by the invigilators steely glare, as she once more squinted at her watch. "You may now open your question papers and commence the examination," she announced. "The very best of luck to you all!"

"And may God have mercy on your souls!" Ivan breathed, as he looked for the first time at the document which could dictate the pattern of the rest of his existence. Following the advice which Ted had forced into the addled brains of his students, and which been reinforced by the sitting of seemingly endless test papers and mock exams during the last three weeks of the three-year course, Ivan read through all ten questions with great care. He studiously read the legend printed at the top of the first page which warned the hapless victims that no marks would be awarded for irrelevant material. Mindful of the tales he had often heard of candidates who had answered the question 'What is dyspepsia'? only, when it was too late and the paper had been handed in, to discover that the question was actually 'What is dyspnoea'? he set about answering the six questions that he felt most comfortable with — 'comfortable' being a relative word!

He was conscious that time had seemingly accelerated, and the half hour periods which he had mentally allocated to each question seemed to only last for five minutes each. He was strangely simultaneously relieved, elated and anxious when he heard the invigilator announce that only five minutes of the exam remained. He had answered six questions, and he had taken time to read them through. He had just crossed the last 'T' and dotted the last 'I' when the invigilator called out,

"Time's up. Please stop writing and close your answer books."

A girl sitting two rows in front of Ivan said, "Oh dear!" and scribbled furiously. The invigilator's face was a mask.

"Stop writing, or I will be obliged to disqualify you!" she said, clearly.

The invigilator strode to the girl's side. "The examination is over — you *must* stop writing!"

The girl cried out in anguish "Please — I only have a couple of lines to write!"

The invigilator snatched the answer book from the desk and tore it into pieces.

The girl cried out in anguish then broke down in tears.

"Will the rest of you please leave the room?" the invigilator said. Ted Jones stepped out of his office into the corridor as Ivan approached. "What's going on in there?" he asked, nodding towards the exam room.

"Some girl carried on writing after the bell," Ivan told him. "The 'Gestapo' lady tore her paper up!"

"Oh dear!" said Ted, thoughtfully. "Still, the rules are the rules, and no one is exempt from them!"

"Bit hard though, isn't it?" Ivan asked.

"Maybe!" said Ted. "But if she couldn't finish the exam in the time allotted, perhaps she's in the wrong job. Nurses are supposed to be organised and competent, and she apparently isn't. It's tough, but that's how it is!"

"I'm not so sure!" Ivan said, rubbing his chin. "After all, the exam is important to her!"

"It's important to all of you!" Ted replied. "But the rest of you had no problem in finishing in time, did you?" He looked at Ivan questioningly.

Ivan turned away and went into the dining room to find Vic and Jock.

The two were sitting at a table drinking tea. "Rum business, wasn't it?" Vic said.

"Aye, I felt a mite sorry for the lassie," Jock drawled.

Ivan kept his thoughts on the subject to himself for the time being. "How did you two get on?" he asked.

"No problem!" said Vic, leaning back in his chair and pushing his lapels forwards with his thumbs. "Easiest exam I've ever failed!"

"As bad as that eh?" Ivan said, with a slight grin. "How about you, Hamish?"

"Who's Hamish?" Jock asked, with feigned indignation. "I thought some of the questions were written in Swahili. Mind, they must have been as bad for everyone."

"Well, I don't know about you two, but I'm going to have a bath, put my suit on and go into town," said Ivan. "Anyone fancy joining me?"

"I'm for that!" Jock agreed. "How about you, Vic?"

"I suppose we may as well drown our sorrows," Vic said. "I thought you were seeing Dawn tonight."

Ivan said, "No, she's gone to visit her aunt in hospital. I said I'd ring her later to let her know how we'd suffered. I was joking at the time, but I'm not so sure now." He was thinking about the girl whose paper had been destroyed.

The three climbed into Jock's old Triumph Mayflower an hour or so later and drove into Derfield. Jock manoeuvred the vehicle into a parking space and switched off the engine. "Where are we going? Any ideas?"

"What about the Crown and Cushion?" Vic asked.

"What about it?" Jock asked, winking at Ivan.

"It's a pub!" said Vic, a little mystified at Jock's rhetoric.

"That's the type of establishment we're seeking," said Ivan. He opened the car door. "Let's sally forth!"

"Aye, Sally fourth after the other three, then for Fat Aggie!" Jock quipped.

"You're incorrigible!" Ivan laughed.

"Ah'm no!" Jock bristled. "I'm Scottish, and proud o' it!"

"You're a twit too!" said Vic, picking up the banter.

"Ah'm a McCracken. Ma grandfather was the McCracken o' Inverary. He was a world champion haggis hunter!" Jock said, puffing out his cheeks with mock indignation.

"Oh gawd!" said Ivan, pained. "He believes it too!"

"It's all the porridge they eat you know?" offered Vic. "It builds up inside them and presses on the base of the brain!"

"Aye, that's true!" Jock agreed. "It can only be relieved by drinking whisky!"

"I've always felt relieved after drinking whisky," Ivan said.

"Well, mind you don't splash your boots then!" Vic said. They were all laughing as they walked into the saloon bar of the Crown and Cushion.

Their laughter died away as they stepped into the room and looked around. The place was totally deserted. The dusty wooden panels lining the walls added to the atmosphere of gloom pervading the room. The name of a long defunct brewing company was painted in red across a murky mirror, which was built into the worm-eaten wooden fittings behind the bar, which was lit by a single bulb hanging from a flyblown glass shade.

The smell of stale beer and cigarette smoke assaulted Ivan's nostrils.

"Blimey! What a dump!" he said.

"Aye, it reminds me of The Gorbals!" Jock growled. "Why did ye' bring us here?" He looked at Vic, accusingly.

"Because, gentlemen, as you will by now have recognised, I am something of a connoisseur of the brewer's art!"

"I thought you told me you were a sufferer of brewer's droop!" Ivan quipped.

"That too!" Vic said, in lofty tones. But tonight, mon freres, you will be well-advised to follow my advice. I do agree, however, that the décor is perhaps a little outmoded."

"Out-clapped, I'd say!" Jock interrupted.

"As I was saying, before this Caledonian Philistine derailed my train of thought." Vic continued, "The place might not be up to much, but the best bitter ale here is nectar. Liquid poetry! The drink of the gods. Nirvana!"

"What you're trying to tell us," Ivan interjected. "Is that the landlord keeps a decent drop of wallop!"

"Correction!" said Vic. "Landlady, not landlord!" He leaned over the bar and yelled, "*Alice*!" at the top of his voice.

"All right! I'm coming! Keep yer 'air on," shouted a female voice from the tap room.

A large, red-faced woman appeared behind the bar. She had a turban on her head fashioned from a scarf, and the stump of a cigarette drooped from her lip, the ash spilling down the front of her grubby floral overall. Ivan thought she looked more like a charwoman than a publican, although he had to admit he had encountered many male landlords who would have made Alice look like a fashion model in comparison.

"Three pints, is it?" she asked, already pulling the first one.

Vic took the drinks from the bar as Alice dispensed them, handing a glass to each of his companions. He watched their faces in anticipation as they took their first draughts of Alice's bitter. Ivan raised the glass to his lips and started to drink. He took an experimental sip first, rolling the beer around his mouth to allow it to reach all of his taste buds. Like Vic, he believed that if a beer was worth drinking, it was worth drinking well. He took another sip, then lifted the glass and downed the rest of the pint in three great gulps, gasping for air and beaming in pleasure as he thumped the glass down on the bar, sated!

"By Gad, Alice!" he gasped. "I don't often take much notice of what he says," indicating Vic, "but that was sheer perfection. I commend you, Madam, on your excellent cellar craft!" He bowed formally to Alice, who's big, ruddy face creased into a grin.

"Go on with yer rubbish!" she laughed, as she refilled the three glasses. "You're as daft as your mate there. I had to ring a taxi to get him home last time he was in here!" She left the bar, chortling merrily.

Ivan looked around the saloon bar again. *It was strange*, he thought, *but the place seemed different now. Sort of cosy and homely*!

"I never did like modern pubs much," he laughed.

"Me neither!" Vic agreed. "Mind you, Murdoch's first law of Boozology states 'the quality of a public house is not to be judged by the quality of its environs, but by the taste of its beer'. That's my basic philosophy of life." He hefted his glass to savour the results of the combined talents of the brewer, who he regretted he would probably never meet, and Alice, who already regretted meeting him!

"Your philosophy is obviously as basic as the rest of you!" Jock offered.

"Ah! Knock not the owner of the head which first guided you to this shrine of dipsimity!" Ivan said, through the bottom of his glass.

"Shrine of what?" Vic asked.

"Dipsimity. A word which I have coined from the Greek 'dipso — to drink'."

"A very good word!" Vic said, his eyes glazed.

"I think sho too!" Jock said, smiling fatuously. "Who'sh round, is it?"

"It'sh yoursh!" Ivan informed him.

"Ah good!" the Scot hiccupped. "I like to pay my corner!"

"You musht be pished!" Vic suggested.

"Musht be what?"

"Pished!" Vic hiccupped and sat down on one of the old wooden settles surrounding the room.

"I've jusht thought of something!" Ivan said, burping.

"Whatsh that?" Vic asked.

"We've got Jock's car, and we're all too pished to drive!"

"Too what?" Jock asked.

"Don't start all that again," Ivan said, testily. "How are we going to get back?"

"We could walk," Jock suggested.

"I couldn't walk to the edge of the pavement just now!" Ivan countered. "No, we'll have to get a taxshi!"

"A what?" Vic countered.

"A taxshi. I'll go and ring for one!" Ivan staggered uncertainly to the coin box phone on the wall of the entrance vestibule. He staggered back a few minutes later, Jock and Vic having downed another pint each of Alice's liquid quintessence in the interim.

"Taxshi's coming!" he announced, picking up what was to be, for now, his last pint of Alice's heavenly brew. The taxi duly arrived, the driver kindly moving Jock's car to the yard at the rear of The Crown And Cushion, with Alice pledged to guard it for him. It had turned out to be quite a night.

Ivan spent the following morning with his head seemingly trapped in the jaws of a vice. As he painfully awoke and swung his feet to the floor, he sat up, muttering the time worn rubric of the severely hung over — 'never again'! His head, seemingly as fragile as a thin wine glass, seemed to shatter into shards as someone pounded on his room door with a battering ram.

"All right! All right!" he moaned, unlatching the door in the hope that he might fall through the floor and be put out of his misery.

Dawn walked in. "God! You look terrible!" she said, trying not to laugh at this pitiful wreck, who she was about to plight her troth to. "Wherever did you get to last night?"

"I don't know!" Ivan groaned. "But wherever it was, I'll never go there again!"

"I've just seen Vic," she said. "He looks as bad as you do. Was Jock there too?"

"Ach! Whist woman, ye're shouting too loud!" said Jock, as he staggered through the door.

"It serves you right — the lot of you!" Dawn scolded. "There's only one good thing about it. You were obviously too drunk to get involved with the female sex!"

"Dinnae mention that word!" Jock groaned. "It could be fatal to someone in my delicate state of health!"

Dawn laughed. "Come on, you pair. You'll feel better after a good breakfast!"

"Oh Satan! Thy name is woman!" Ivan moaned, allowing himself to be led to the dining room like a lamb to the slaughter.

The powers of recovery of the human body are quite wondrous, and an hour later, after a breakfast of hot, sweet tea and thickly buttered toast, Ivan's only reminder of his recent close encounter with the Grim Reaper was a dull but persistent throbbing of his skull. He was sitting in the sometimes inaptly named 'quiet room' of the nurses' home when Ted Jones came in.

"Hello!" he said, looking at Ivan's pallid complexion. "Have you been ill?"

"Severely!" Ivan said. "It was a near thing until nursey here saved me!"

"A case of overindulgence in the juice of the malt and hop!" Dawn laughed.

"Ah! I see! Ted laughed. "Serves you right then! I've no sympathy for you but perhaps a little empathy!"

"That's what they all tell me!" Ivan said.

"I would have thought you might have delayed the wake until after the orals and practical's," he said, puffing his ancient and smelly tobacco pipe into life. "Have you had the letter telling you where they're being held yet?"

"Nottingham," Ivan said. "You know, the old place up on the hill?"

"Ah yes! I know!" said Ted. "I went there last year to give a lecture on aversion therapy in alcoholism!"

"Ouch! Did you have to?" Ivan laughed, beginning to re-join the human race.

Ted grinned. "I think you'll be OK. Do you know who the examiners are yet?"

"No idea!" Ivan said. "Does it matter?"

"I'll say!" Ted chortled. "They all stick to the rules, of course, but some stick faster than others."

"What are the signs to watch out for? Ivan asked.

Ted looked pensive. "Beware the happy smiling ones. They'll fail you without compunction. The sour featured ones are tortured by the gravity of their task. They might look grim, but underneath those stony features, there is often a tender heart. You can never really tell of course. That's why the nine or ten weeks' wait for the result is such fun for those of us, who having been taught, now teach! I love to watch them suffer as the fateful 'day of the postman' draws nigh!"

"Is sadism an entry requirement for training as a tutor?" Ivan asked.

"No! It just develops as a mental defence mechanism, as a result of witnessing repeated failure amongst your students. Fortunately, during my many years in my exalted position, I've only lost a few, and they mostly passed their resits. As I said — I think you'll be OK!" Ted rose to leave, wisely quitting the conversation whilst he was still ahead!

"Are you worried about the practicals?" Dawn asked.

Ivan smiled faintly, now beginning to feel that he may survive. "Not really. I've become somewhat philosophical about the whole thing now. Your turn will come, next year! If I have failed, I'll just have to take another shot at it. I do begrudge paying two lots of exam fees though." He thought for a while. "I know what we *could* do!" he said, tentatively.

"What's that?" she mused.

"I could stay at home and do the housework and you could be the breadwinner."

"No! No!" Dawn howled. "Don't send me down the mine Daddy! I'm too young and tender!"

"That ye are, me dear!" Ivan laughed, lecherously. He grabbed at Dawn, who ran out of the room squealing, with Ivan pursuing her.

"At it again, are you?" said Vic, as he came round the corner of the corridor.

Two weeks later, the three pals sat apprehensively waiting to be called in to the practical examination room. This was where they would have to prove their competence by setting up trays and trolleys in preparation for a number of medical and minor surgical procedures like wound dressings, injection and similar 'physical' nursing duties. They would also be asked to bandage the simulated wounds of the brave patient who had volunteered to be the 'dummy' for this particular group of hopefuls to work on. They would be subjected to a barrage of questions from the examiner in the room, then onto two more — possibly a doctor and a nurse, who would be carrying out the oral (sometimes referred to as 'Vivers') examinations.

The principal tutor of the Nurse Training School of the hospital which was hosting the exams that day addressed the candidates en masse before the actual exams commenced.

"You will enter the practical examination room in pairs," she intoned. "You will be met by the examiners as you enter the room and will be asked to present your examination cards. As at your written examination, any attempts at cheating will disqualify you, and you must stop whatever you are doing and leave the room at the end of the allotted time. A bell will ring at the cut-off point, and no marks will thereafter be awarded. Any attempt to continue after the bell will also disqualify you. You will be expected to complete any tasks given to you by the examiner within the time available. The examiners will allow sufficient time for the competent completion of these tasks."

Ivan remembered the unfortunate incident at the end of the written exam, and he hoped that he would not be witness to a similar occurrence today.

The principal tutor and one of the examiners put all the numbered slips of paper into a biscuit tin. The tutor shook the tin and offered it to the examiner to pull out the first pair of slips. Ivan had hoped that his name would be drawn with someone from The Meadows, preferably Jock or Vic, but he was disappointed. A stockily built, swarthy little chap with glasses turned out to be his partner. In the interests of politeness, Ivan crossed the room and offered his hand.

"By 'eck, I'm reet nervous, tha knows!" his partner said, in a thick Yorkshire accent.

"Well, I should try to calm down a bit," Ivan suggested. "You'll have me getting nervous otherwise!"

"Is it your first time?" the other fellow asked.

"Yes! And you?"

"Ee! No lad! This'll be my third go at it. I can't help it, tha knaws. I know my stuff all reet, but as soon as I get in there, I go all to pieces!" He took out a handkerchief and mopped his brow with it.

"What's your name?" Ivan asked.

"Eddie. What's yours?"

"Mine's Ivan. Now look Eddie, if we try to work as a team, we'll help each other, but if we don't get things organised, we'll only get in each other's way and make a mess of it!"

"Oh aye, tha's reet theer lad" Eddie agreed, enthusiastically. "I said summat similar t' last feller I went in with, but he didn't seem to hear what I was saying to him. At least, if he did, he didn't understand me!"

"What was he like?" Ivan asked.

"He was a nice enough chap in his own way," Eddie informed him. "But I never quite know how to take these Indian fellows, tha knaws. They nod and smile at thee, and tha thinks they've understood thee, but tha's never reet sure?"

Ivan smiled at the image of some poor Indian chap, probably frightened out of his wits by the importance of the occasion, trying to interpret Eddie's thick Yorkshire accent, and with typical Indian manners, being too polite to ask for clarification of Eddie's intentions. Ivan decided that this situation called for resolve.

"I'll tell you what!" Ivan said. "When they give us the situation, you go and collect the equipment and I'll get the patient and the bed ready — you know, screened off etcetera!" That way, we'll be able to get everything organised!"

"Aye, OK Ivan!" Eddie said. "I can see you and me's going to get along just fine!" He grinned, nervously, again wiping the perspiration from his forehead. "Just fine!" he muttered, wringing his hands in a vain attempt to quell the panic rising in his breast.

The pair who had been immediately before Ivan and Eddie on the list had now been inside the examination room for some fifteen minutes, and Ivan realised that it would soon be his turn to 'face the music' with or without Eddie's help. He did not dare to mention the passage of time to Eddie, who looked as though he may run from the building at any moment. At length, the door to the room was opened and the other pair came out, obviously relieved that their ordeal was now over. The invigilator beckoned to Ivan and Eddie, who rose and stepped through the door. Ivan was now conscious of his own feelings of anxiety, but when he looked at Eddie, who bore an expression of abject terror, he realised that he was more concerned about Eddie distracting him from the task in hand than he was about any of his own possible shortcomings.

He kept trying to inwardly convince himself that nothing could go wrong. After all, he had been thoroughly trained for three years in anticipation of just this moment, and Ted Jones had reassured all the students that they were now perfectly prepared for the examinations. So, if that was the case, why did he now feel more vulnerable and unprepared than at any time during his training?

The examiner greeted them with what was obviously intended to be a reassuring smile, but Ivan was reminded of Ted Jones' words to 'beware the happy, smiling examiner', but he ascribed this to Ted's somewhat warped sense of humour.

"Now, gentlemen!" the examiner, a red-faced chap in his mid-fifties said. "I'd like you to imagine that this poor chap." He indicated the patient in the bed. "Has fallen down the stairs and fractured his right tibia and fibula. We'll assume that you have managed to get him into the bed without further mishap, and all I would like you to do now is to immobilise the fracture in preparation for his transfer to the general hospital, where, hopefully, the fracture will be manipulated and reduced. I'll give you five minutes to prepare."

As previously agreed, Ivan went behind the screens to the bedside, whilst Eddie, Ivan assumed, took a trolley round the room to collect the various pads, splints and bandages which would be required to immobilise the imaginary injury. Ivan felt a little happier now, as he knew that the situation that they had been given was so fundamental that even Eddie should have found it relatively simple. He asked the patient his name, and found out when and where he had fallen, and where the main area of discomfort was. He had two main reasons for eliciting this information. One was that he was sure that the examiner would question him along these lines, and the other was that he knew that the patients who often acted as 'models' for the examinations knew more than the panic-stricken nurses who were attempting to demonstrate their skills upon them.

Ivan turned the bedclothes back and covered the patient's legs with a light sheet in anticipation of Eddie's arrival with the trolley. He then ventured to look over the screens for the now overdue Eddie. To Ivan's horror, Eddie was pushing the empty trolley round and round the room, his wide eyes fixed with a terrified stare behind his thick, heavily rimmed spectacles.

"Pssst!" Ivan hissed. This had the effect of breaking Eddie's terror filled reverie, causing him to rapidly halt his amnesic perambulations. Fortunately, he retained just enough presence of mind to realise that he should join Ivan at the bedside. Ivan discretely relieved Eddie of the trolley and set off to complete his partner's forlorn quest for the requisite materials. In a matter of minutes, he was back behind the screens with the now laden trolley, and he was ready to begin the procedure.

The examiner now joined them behind the screens. After what seemed to Ivan to be hours of pushing, tugging and grabbing behind Eddie's obvious lack of technique, he was reasonably assured that the leg was now comfortably splinted, and that the bandages were neither too tight as to add gangrene to the patient's condition, or so slack that they would fall off, to say nothing of the poor fellow's leg, at the slightest movement. Then came the time to make up the bed over the injured patient, an important part of the procedure, which the examiner would observe at close hand.

Ivan addressed Eddie, in quiet tones. "We'll put a sheet over his legs, then a bed cradle over the fractured leg before we replace the blankets."

"Eh, Whassat?" was Eddie's response.

"I said, we'll put a sheet over his legs, then a bed cradle to support the weight of the blankets," Ivan repeated.

"Nay lad!" Eddie began. "He'll catch his death o' cawd if tha does that!" to Ivan's shocked disbelief. "'E'll be in shock, sithee? 'E's bound to feel t' cawd if 'e's in shock!"

"Of course, he's in shock!" Ivan hissed trying to remain calm. "He's got a broken leg, and if we put heavy blankets on his legs, he'll go deeper into shock because of the pain, won't he!"

"'Ow's that?" Eddie said, sounding like Freddie Truman.

Ivan looked in desperation at the examiner, who merely smiled. "Look — let's do it my way, then if you're right, you'll pass and I'll fail!"

"Oh aye!" said Eddie, vacantly.

Eventually, the bed was made up as Ivan had wanted. The examiner pulled back the bedclothes and checked the splint and the tension of the bandages.

"Right, gentlemen!" he smiled, betraying no sign at all of his thoughts. "Now!" He turned to Eddie. "I'd be grateful if you would set up a trolley for male catheterisation, please."

"Aye, righto then!" said Eddie, almost stumbling over the rubber pipe from an oxygen cylinder as he blundered around the room.

The examiner turned to Ivan, still smiling, and showing no sign of what his thoughts were, although Ivan thought he could just detect the faintest sign of a pained look in the man's eyes as he followed Eddie's crashing progress amongst the equipment.

"Would you tell me please — if you had been instructing a junior nurse in this procedure, how would you have suggested making the bed up?"

Ivan felt a little uneasy. He had been quite convinced that he had been right at the time, but he wondered why the examiner had raised the subject again.

"In exactly the same way!" he said, boldly.

"I see. Thank you!" He smiled, remaining totally inscrutable. "Now, would you be kind enough to set up a trolley for intravenous infusion?"

Ivan brightened at this request, as he had often set up similar trolleys during his training, under supervision from Bob Bracewell and others. He busily set about his task of loading the upper and lower shelves of the trolley, and bringing a drip stand to its side. The examiner asked him a few fairly basic questions about the management of intravenous infusions, and Ivan was surprised when the bell rang to mark the end of the exam in seemingly short time. As he left the room, Eddie caught his foot against Ivan's carefully prepared trolley, sending the contents skittering across the floor. Ivan grimaced and left him to it, relieved that this part of his own ordeal was now over.

He took a seat in the waiting room, as previously instructed, to await being summoned into another room for the 'oral'. He felt a little easier about this section, as he would be alone in the room with the two examiners, without having Eddie to contend with.

He was, at length, called in by one of the examiners, who only addressed him by his exam number, preserving anonymity. Ivan took the seat in front of the desk. The examiners — a man and a lady — sat on the other side. He recognised the lady as being the Matron of one of the hospitals whose catchment area joined that of The Meadows. Whilst he had not met the lady before, he had been told that she was a kindly soul, a description which was borne out by her winning smile. The other examiner informed Ivan that he was a Consultant Psychiatrist from the hospital which was today hosting the examination.

It was the doctor who began the exam. "Tell me?" he said. "What do you think about homosexuals?"

"In what respect? Ivan asked.

"In any respect."

"Well, not being that way inclined myself, I don't have any strong feelings about them in any way."

"How do you know you're not?" the doctor asked, grimly.

"Well, I think I can be reasonably confident," Ivan faltered.

The doctor cut in swiftly. "Oh! So, it's to do with confidence, is it?"

Ivan was beginning to feel more than a little nonplussed. "I am a little unsure about your line of questioning, with respect!" he said.

"OK!" the doctor said quietly. "I'll rephrase my question. Now, let's suppose that someone was admitted to your ward suffering from depression — OK?" He looked at Ivan quizzically.

Ivan nodded. "Yes, I think I'm with you so far!"

"Good!" said the doctor. "Now! Suppose that when he's been in hospital for a few days, he feels like talking. In the course of a conversation about the weather, gardening, football or some other subject completely unrelated to his sexual identity, he decides that you are sufficiently approachable to suddenly tell you that the real reason for his depression is not the financial difficulty he told the doctor was the root of his misery, but that he had begun to experience sexual thoughts about men. He might go on to say that these thoughts have begun to pervade his whole thinking, and that everything he did during the course of a day seems somehow to remind him of his problem. Are you still with me?"

Ivan nodded his assent.

"Right, now then! What are you going to do?"

Ivan thought for a few seconds. "I think I'd probably start by asking him if he thought that I was the best person to talk to about the subject."

"Oh?" And why would you ask him that?"

Ivan replied, "Well, it may be that the doctor would be the right person to discuss it with."

The Psychiatrist looked a little impatient, knitting his brow as he spoke. "No, that's not what I want to hear!" he said. "Look — this patient has decided that he wants to tell *you* about this problem, not the doctor. Now, how do you feel about this?"

Ivan was beginning to feel a little nonplussed also a little irritated. "Well, I must confess that privately, I may feel a little worried about why he had decided to confide in me rather than someone better qualified. This may, I suppose, be because of the uncomfortable feelings which arise in most of the male population whenever the subject of homosexuality is raised. But despite that, I hope that I would be able to provide him with the 'listening ear' that he was seeking. I would try to persuade him to be as honest with the doctor as he had been with me. What I'm trying to say, I suppose, is that whatever my own feelings and prejudices may be, I would try very hard to prevent them from becoming a barrier between myself and the patient, who obviously needs a confidante."

"Good!" the doctor smiled. "Now we seem to understand each other. But what *about* this chap? Supposing he tells you not to breathe a word of what he's said to anyone else. What would you do then?"

Ivan was a little more relaxed. "This is a common dilemma," he said. "Patients need to feel that they can speak to nurses and other staff in total confidence, and sometimes, a nurse finds that this puts him or her in a difficult position. If I couldn't persuade the patient to tell the doctor what was really troubling him of his own volition, I may offer to act as his 'go between' or advocate in approaching the doctor."

The doctor looked impressed. "Would there be any circumstances in which you may decide to go against the patient's wishes and actually discuss the situation with the doctor?"

Ivan replied, "This would depend entirely upon my relationship with the doctor. If I felt that I could rely entirely upon the doctor's total discretion, which is the normal situation, I would confide the information to him. If, on the other hand, I felt that by doing so I would destroy the patient's confidence in me, I would have to decide which course of action was in the patient's best interest. I must admit though, this situation has not arisen for me so far." He looked the doctor directly in the eye. "It's called 'professional judgment' I think!"

The doctor grinned widely. "Fair enough!" he said. "All yours, Matron!"

The Matron confined her questions entirely to Ivan's understanding of the mental health act, to his profound relief. Once again, the bell rang to signify the end if the examination in what seemed to Ivan to be very short time. His ordeal was now at an end!

As had been his custom for many years on the evening after an examination, Ted Jones joined the students in The Nags Head. He didn't make a regular habit of drinking with his 'flock', but he had found in the past that some of them may wish to talk through their experiences. Some may need their confidence boosted and some simply wanted to let their hair down. In many ways, these groups intertwined, the students often passing though all three phases during the course of the evening.

Much ribald banter was exchanged, Ted fearing at one stage that he was in danger of being 'de-bagged' in time honoured fashion. Having averted this disaster, he made it his business to speak quietly to each student in turn, evoking their fears, doubts and in many cases, their optimism. Ivan told him about what had seemed to be the Psychiatrist's strange fixation.

Ted looked pensive. "It's difficult to know what he was trying to find out, of course, but I do know that a lot of the examiners just lately have tried to explore the candidate's ability to put their own feelings in a secondary position to those of the patient. I think it's 'fair game' in the main, but I can see how the 'victim' may feel it was a little unfair."

"Yes, I suppose that's it," Ivan said. "It was quite perplexing at the time though."

Ted grinned. "There is one other possibility of course!"

"Oh, what's that?" Ivan asked, in innocence.

"Perhaps he fancied you!" Ted guffawed, as Ivan poured the last quarter of his pint over the tutor's head!

CHAPTER EIGHTEEN

The exams over, Ivan, Vic and Jock once again found themselves on night duty. It had been the custom at The Meadows for many years for the students to be placed on nights for three months at the end of each year of training, and the end of the crucial third term was no exception. There was, however, a final one-week bloc in the school of nursing before they were plunged into darkness.

This bloc was mainly intended to help the students through the eight weeks wait for the exam results, in an attempt to prevent them from too much 'brooding' during the long, dark, winter night shifts.

As his last ministry to the largest majority of each set, who would receive the news that they had passed, Ted Jones tried to prepare them for the arrival of the fateful buff envelope, franked with the insignia of the general nursing council, which would bear within its' manilla folds, that which they simultaneously hoped and dreaded to read.

"You will find, ladies and gentlemen, that your emotions will alternate between maniacal optimism and darkest dread during the next few weeks, as the doyens of our profession plough through thousands of papers, attempting, often much against their better judgement, to pass as many of you as they can without turning loose a bunch of bungling incompetents upon the unsuspecting and vulnerable members of the public, whose only crime, to warrant such an awful fate, was to be unwise enough to seek relief from their sufferings in a hospital where you have at last begun to learn the real stuff of nursing."

"Were this not bad enough for them, they will little suspect, in their blissful ignorance, that not only are you likely to inflict upon their already tortured flesh the results of your mistaken judgments, but that you are now fully qualified to do so, and that henceforth, should you poison them with wrongly administered medicines, or infect their tissues with badly given injections, you will be able to hide behind the impenetrable curtain of something vaguely described as 'professional judgment'. Such is the tangled web that it is my misfortune to weave twice a year." He held his head in mock despair.

"Cheerful sod, isn't he?" Vic asked, with high disdain for his mentor's once lauded status.

"Yeah!" Ivan replied. "Really fills you with confidence!"

The occasion had been their last visit (they hoped!) to the Nurse Training School, to collect their books and other memorabilia of three years that were now behind them and enshrined in memory. Ivan went to his room and placed them untidily on his dressing table, and then, thinking better of it, gathered them up and placed them neatly on the little bookshelves which each staff room was provided. Until now, the shelves had been filled with old newspapers and slightly Fescennine magazines, which Dawn had consigned to the dustbin once the relationship reached the room visiting stage.

With a last, thoughtful look at the tattered spines of the books in their new resting place, he switched off the light and closed the door. He met Jock and Vic in their usual semi recumbent post prandial torpor, having supped on eggs, beans, sausages and chips, an ill-conceived and misanthropic act before a night shift.

"Well, here we go again, sacrificing ourselves to the night!" Ivan said, as he sat down with his own plate of fried flatulence.

"You know, here's an auld saying!" Jock drawled.

"What's that?" Vic asked, instantly regretting having done so.

"Ainly policemen, burglars, prostitutes and nurses work nights, weekends and bank holidays! Fie, it'd be braw tae wurruk shopoors!"

"What are shopoors?" Ivan asked.

Vic said, "I think what our Caledonian friend means, if I have correctly construed it, is that it would be rather nice to work shop hours, as normal people do!"

"Ach!" Jock spluttered. "If we were normal people, we'd no be aboot here the noo!"

"Yes, I suppose you're right, Ivan said. "Still, wouldn't do for us all to be the same, would it?" So, saying he rose from the table and strode off towards Male Nine, his placement for the night. As he walked, he thought over the possibilities for his future. If he had passed the exam, he would be able to marry Dawn. Pushing aside the instinctive dread that thoughts of marriage had instilled in the breasts of young men since the dawn of time, he found that he quite liked the idea of settling down, safe in the knowledge that his qualification would always keep him in employment, providing he had managed to convince the examiners of his prowess.

The night passed without notable event, and Ivan re-joined his companions at the breakfast table. All three of them were feeling that bone aching, all pervading tiredness which staying awake all night can produce. From his previous experience, Ivan knew that if he did not get to sleep within an hour, it would be days or possibly weeks before his body stopped objecting to the assault upon its circadian rhythm which this first night shift always brought. Gaining the sanctity of his room, he gratefully slipped between the sheets and drifted into slumber.

Ten minutes later, he was wrenched back into wakefulness by a sound which suggested that Armageddon had arrived. Squinting through the curtains, he was dismayed to see a gang of workmen digging up the road outside the hostel, a pneumatic drill being the source of the racket. Pulling on his dressing gown, he staggered out into the hall, meeting Jock and Vic in similar attire as he did so. They went out into the road, but their protestations to the workmen fell on deaf ears.

Gathering back in the relative calm of Jock's room, they discussed the shattering of their peace with much invective. They were about to go back to their rooms to try to sleep when Vic suddenly brightened.

"I know!" he said. "Let's go out!"

"Out?" the other pair chorused, convinced that their friend had lost the few marbles he still possessed.

"Yes — out!" Vic said, enthusiastically. "Let's go out into the country. It's a nice day and we could take sleeping bags and kip down in a field. Anything's better than this row!"

"You know?" Ivan mused, "maybe he's got something there! Let's try it!"

An hour later, the detached observer may have been somewhat baffled to see these bleary-eyed young men climb out of an ancient Triumph Mayflower — Jock's pride and joy — and troop off into a wood clutching three borrowed sleeping bags and pillows. Indeed, the detached observer would have been even more baffled to see Vic yawn, wind up his alarm clock and instantly fall asleep amongst the trees.

Our observer, had he stuck to his task, would have been sure that he was right in his decision to remain detached, if he had stayed in the vicinity long enough to hear a string of Anglo-Saxon invective in a broad Scottish accent as a famer in a nearby field started up his tractor and began ploughing.

"Ach! It's no right at 'a!'" Jock growled. "Here we are, three guardians of the nation's sanity and we're being driven mad by the remainder of the human race!"

"It might be going a bit far to condemn all of humanity," Vic ventured, "but in our present circumstances, it does seem that most of the population of Britain is out to get us!"

"Ach awa' and boil ye're toot!" Jock roared, grabbing his sleeping bag and heading back to the car.

"What did he say?" Vic asked, dumbfounded.

"I think he was suggesting a method by which you may improve your sensitivity towards your fellow man!" Ivan replied.

"Do you mean I've upset him?" Vic asked

"Come on!" Ivan said. "If we don't catch up with Haggis, he's likely to drive off and leave us here!"

"Aye, and it'd serve ye pair of Sassenach bastards right if I did, too!" Jock grunted.

"What have we done?" Vic asked, as Ivan kicked him on the shin

"I've just realised something!" Ivan ventured.

"By God — the boy thinks!" said Jock, sarcastically.

"What have you realised?" Vic asked, disconsolately.

"They're open!" Ivan said, pointing at his watch.

Jock stopped, transfixed. "When did you realise that?" he asked.

"About ten seconds ago," Ivan said.

Jock grabbed him by the lapels. "Do you mean to tell me that you realised that the pubs were open a whole ten seconds ago, and you've only just got around to telling us, after I have been

302

kind enough to place my personal limousine at your disposal?"

"Well, you know me!" Ivan said, brightly. "I didn't want to spring it on you too soon in case the excitement proved too much for your delicate constitutions."

"Well, that's very thoughtful of you," Vic said, gratuitously, playfully returning the kick on the shin, "but there were really no grounds for your concern. They all got back into the car, bound for The Nags Head.

Jock's suggestion that they should go to The Nags Head proved to be wise, as by the time they left the pub at mid-day, none of them were fit to drive. They left the Mayflower on the pub's car park and staggered back to the hostel. Gaining the safety of their rooms, they all got into their beds and subsided into unconsciousness, oblivious to the continuing noise that had driven them out earlier in the day.

Some hours later, Ivan drifted back into the land of the living. Opening his eyes, he was, at first, convinced that he was dead. He was chilled to the bone, surrounded by darkness and completely disoriented in both time and space. Having established that he was, in fact, alive, the next problem was to establish where he was. His former fears of being dead returned briefly when right hand touched another hand which felt cadaverously cold and unresponsive. He now believed that his companions had found his prostrate form and that they had placed him in the hospital mortuary in the mistaken belief that he had expired. On further examination, however, he discovered that he had found his own left hand, which was numb from being laid on. His eyes had adjusted to the dark, and he was able, on realising that he was in his room, to locate the light switch.

Turning the light on proved to be unwise, as he was gripped by a blinding headache as his beleaguered brain reacted to the sudden stimulus. Staggering to the bedside locker, he grasped his alarm clock and stared at its dial, unable at first to comprehend its message. With a gasp of mixed horror and incredulity, he realised that it was eleven o'clock and that he should have been on duty two hours ago.

"Oh, God!" he exclaimed, sitting gingerly on the bed, the blankets of which were on the floor, explaining his coldness. He staggered to the mirror on the shaving cabinet, an act that he instantly regretted on perceiving his features. His eyes were sunken in their sockets, the whites suffused and bloodshot.

He pushed out his tongue, but he could see no sign of the feathers and broken glass which he could quite plainly taste. Ascribing this phenomenon to the quality of the beer at The Nags

Head, (a fairly accurate assumption) he washed, shaved and dressed, an operation which seemed to take hours to complete. With a last look at his wrecked quarters, he set out for his ward, determined to renounce the evils of the demon drink and rebuild his shattered life. He found a message, on arrival there, to see Wally Brown, in his office.

Standing on the office carpet, alongside Jock and Vic, who had also reported late for duty, feeling suitably chaste after the 'rollocking' that Wally handed out to each of them, Ivan resolved that never again would he indulge in alcohol.

As he met Jock and Vic in The Nags Head the following evening, Ivan reflected upon the events of the previous twenty-four hours.

"You know?" he said to Vic, as Jock re-joined them from the bar with three foaming pints, "that was a very close-run thing!"

"Indeed, it was!" Jock said, as they raised their glasses.

"Cheers!", Vic said.

"Cheers!" the others responded, quaffing deeply!

The weeks crawled by, and as Ted Jones had predicted, the emotions of the examinees alternated between high hopes and wretched pessimism about the impending results. Ivan's own thoughts had passed through several of these cycles, and he found, on the morning that the results were to be revealed, he was in a sort of 'no man's land' between the two extremes. Reasonably assured about his efforts in the written paper, the spectre of the strange interview with the doctor in the oral still haunted him. Accompanied by Jock and Vic and the other examinees, he tried to quell the rising panic in his breast as the waited in Mr Hunting's office for the Chief Male Nurse and Ted Jones to arrive with the envelopes. In keeping with tradition, Mr Hunting would pass an envelope to each of the examinees who were resident at the hospital. Later, a similar scene would be played out in the Matron's office for the female nurses.

With Mr Hunting's permission, Dawn had joined them, and she reassuringly squeezed Ivan's hand as they waited. At length, the door opened and Ted and Mr Hunting walked in with the envelopes in a sealed box. The box was opened, and the 'Chief' solemnly handed an envelope to each of those waiting.

Ivan, Jock and Vic looked at each other, and simultaneously opened their letters.

"Dear Mr Reader." Ivan read. "We are pleased to inform you—!" He didn't read the rest.

"I've passed!" whooped Ivan.

"So have I!" said Jock.

"Me too!" Vic said.

"Congratulations lads!" Mr Hunting said, shaking each one warmly by the hand.

"I always thought you'd do it!" Ted grinned.

Ivan breathed a sigh of relief. "Phew! I'm glad that's over!" he said.

"Over?" Ted said. "You haven't even started yet!"

As the laughter subsided, Dawn put reached into her handbag. "Now, I've got some envelopes to hand out," she smiled, handing one each to Jock, Vic, Ted and a surprised Mr Hunting.

"What are they?" Ted asked.

Dawn took a firm hold on Ivan's arm. "Wedding invitations!" she said.